Research Design in Social Work

SAGE was founded in 1965 by Sara Miller McCune to support the dissemination of usable knowledge by publishing innovative and high-quality research and teaching content. Today, we publish over 900 journals, including those of more than 400 learned societies, more than 800 new books per year, and a growing range of library products including archives, data, case studies, reports, and video. SAGE remains majority-owned by our founder, and after Sara's lifetime will become owned by a charitable trust that secures our continued independence.

Los Angeles | London | New Delhi | Singapore | Washington DC | Melbourne

Research Design in Social Work

Qualitative and Quantitative Methods

Anne Campbell, Brian J. Taylor & Anne McGlade

 |

Series Editors:
Jonathan Parker and Greta Bradley

Learning Matters
An imprint of SAGE Publications Ltd
1 Oliver's Yard
55 City Road
London EC1Y 1SP

SAGE Publications Inc.
2455 Teller Road
Thousand Oaks, California 91320

SAGE Publications India Pvt Ltd
B 1/I 1 Mohan Cooperative Industrial Area
Mathura Road
New Delhi 110 044

SAGE Publications Asia-Pacific Pte Ltd
3 Church Street
#10-04 Samsung Hub
Singapore 049483

Editor: Kate Wharton
Production editor: Chris Marke
Marketing manager: Camille Richmond
Cover design: Wendy Scott
Typeset by: C&M Digitals (P) Ltd, Chennai, India
Printed and bound by CPI Group (UK) Ltd, Croydon, CR0 4YY

Library of Congress Control Number: 2016944012

British Library Cataloguing in Publication Data

A catalogue record for this book is available from the British Library

ISBN 978-1-4462-7124-7(pbk)
ISBN 978-1-4462-7123-0

Contents

About the authors

Anne Campbell is Lecturer in Social Work at Queens University, Belfast. She is responsible for co-ordinating a Master's programme in Social Work studies and is also involved in teaching social work students at Undergraduate level. She has supervised and mentored a wide range of research students at Undergraduate, Masters and PHD levels over a number of years. She is also involved in developing knowledge-based and interactive e- learning tools for practice, research and social work education. She is currently active in research on drug and alcohol issues within regional and international contexts and online applications for social work practice. Anne is co-director of the drug and alcohol research network at Queens (DARN).

Brian J. Taylor is Professor of Social Work at Ulster University in Northern Ireland, where he has the lead role for research in social work. He spent 10 years in practice and 15 years in professional training and organisation development in social work before moving to the university. He teaches research methods to Ph.D. students and to experienced social workers undertaking postgraduate, post-qualifying study. He was module coordinator for an innovative *Introduction to Evidence Based Practice* module on the B.Sc. qualifying social work programme. Brian leads the university social work research cluster on Decision, Assessment, Risk and Evidence Studies and is the primary organiser of a biennial international symposium on this topic. He was a founder Board Member of the European Social Work Research Association, and is an honorary Senior Fellow of the School for Social Care Research of the National Institute for Health Research, London.

Anne McGlade has been Social Care Research Lead for the Social Care and Children's Directorate, Health and Social Care Board since October 2013. She is the lead on the development of the Research and Continuous Improvement Strategy (2015–2020) In Pursuit of Excellence in Evidence Informed Social Work Services in Northern Ireland. She has a long-standing career working in research and evaluation research in health and social care and other settings in England and Northern Ireland. She has a keen interest in the needs of older people, people with disabilities and people from black and minority ethnic groups. She has undertaken and published a range of research studies in these areas. Her interest in equality and human rights led to a career spanning a number of years as an adviser to a range of health and social care organisations. She is also a visiting lecturer and co-tutor on two post-qualifying programmes for social workers at Ulster University: the Application of Research Methods in Social Work and the Evidence Informed Professional and Organisation.

Introduction

The undertaking of an empirical research project at undergraduate or postgraduate level is a difficult but rewarding task which empowers the candidate through a development of her research skills and knowledge, whilst generating new and important research findings for the social work profession. However, the multi-level knowledge exchange reaches far beyond the bolstering of academic and practice knowledge. Indeed in many cases, the undergraduate/postgraduate researcher produces findings which improve an aspect of service provision and ultimately make a difference to the lives of service users, carers, families and communities.

The following chapters aim to encourage potential researchers to take up the positive and reciprocally rewarding challenge of taking a research idea and formulating a project to realise a change in practice policy or procedure. Invariably, the research idea is most often rooted in the prospective researcher's deep passion for change or as a result of their discovery of a gap in the literature or to inform practice at a local or regional level.

However, the passion for research is often dampened somewhat when the student is faced with the myriad of research paradigms, approaches and methodologies which they must navigate at the beginning of the often long and arduous, but eventually satisfying, research journey.

Subsequent to the choosing of the research subject, students are also faced with a plethora of tasks, including choosing the appropriate research methodology and negotiating the many associated sampling techniques. They must then consider a range of data analysis frameworks and the task of concisely summarising the information in a readable and coherent format.

Stages of the research process
Choice of research topic

The cyclical and iterative process of the research journey begins with the choice of project subject area. This is often influenced by the student's fervency for a specific area of practice or as a result of a lack of specific information on the efficacy of an intervention with a certain service user group or the effects of a recent regional policy on service provision. For example, a recent project considered the efficacy of a systemic family therapy programme in practice with juvenile offenders and their families. The project title was selected due to the research student's work interest in the area and his practice knowledge of what he perceived as the efficacy of the project aims and objectives. Another example demonstrated the student researcher's interest in the area of social work placement provision. The student chose to consider the undergraduate social work perceptions of voluntary sector placements in comparison with statutory placements in a social work degree programme. In both cases, the researchers chose subjects which piqued their interest as a result of personal practice experience and provided an impetus and added enthusiasm for the research path that lay ahead.

Some points to remember when choosing a topic

1. Choose a subject that interests you otherwise it may prove difficult to sustain the momentum.

2. Select an area where other research has been carried out as it will provide a context to your project whilst providing enough research and additional literature to substantiate your discussion.

3. Do not choose a research question that is too wide – for example, how do older people cope with bereavement? Rather focus the title to how do older people cope with isolation in the short term following the death of a partner/spouse? Or, what service provision is available for older people to address loneliness in the aftermath of a partner bereavement?

4. How will the research add to the body of knowledge in this subject area and how may it be considered within the context of national and international research findings?

See **Chapter 2** for further discussion on types of study question and the strengths and appropriateness of different research designs for a range of research questions.

Literature review

The literature review is a core component of the research process as it lays the theoretical and policy foundation for the subject of study whilst substantiating the rationale for choice of the subject area. It must be clearly structured from the outset and follow a specific search strategy as explained in Chapter 1.

The findings from relevant studies should be analysed and arranged according to themes and sub-themes that emanate from the data and not simply reported in a regimental fashion. In addition, a summary of findings should be presented and linked specifically to the aims and objectives of the student research project. Over the years of supervising students, it has become clear that those individuals who take the time to sift through the data in a meaningful fashion and extract the themes accordingly tend to have a better grasp of the research objectives and relative research design.

See **Chapter** 1 for further analysis of the formulation and creation of a literature review that is relevant to the subject area and how to present the review in a coherent framework.

Research design

The design should follow very clearly from the research aim and objectives. The aim should be clear and the objectives linked specifically to the methodology. How will each objective be directly translated to a strand of the methodological approach?

If you are selecting a qualitative approach, state clearly how this will meet the particular objectives and how the tools chosen will gather data that is relevant to your objectives. For example, how will data gathered from focus groups illuminate your research aim or how will findings from semi-structured interviews provide you with the necessary data to build your findings and discussion in a meaningful fashion?

Likewise, if you are choosing a quantitative approach, select a research tool which will gather data that will be useful at the analysis phase. This may appear to be a common-sense approach but some students compile a questionnaire and do not think about how the data it generates will be analysed or what findings it will produce to answer the research question. For example, one recent student constructed a questionnaire and realised that she had collected a series of prose-like answers that did not equate with her original objective of rating her respondents' views on alcohol and mental health. Therefore, she was unable to consider associations between, for example, the respondents' length of time in post and their views on daily recommended amounts (the latter variable should have used ranked data such as disagree/ unsure/agree rather than an open-ended question).

Some points to remember in research design

1. Remember to clearly delineate between the research objectives and the methodology as outlined above.
2. State whether the research is qualitative, quantitative or employs a mixed methodological approach.
3. Choose your research tools carefully as they will dictate the type of data that you will generate.
4. Think ahead to the analysis stage now. It is crucial that you are left with data that is manageable and clearly provides information which will meet the needs of the research objectives.

Chapters 2, 4 and **5** will clearly demonstrate how this can be done via the provision of a rationale for choice of design, discussion of a number of methodological approaches and the research tools relevant to the chosen method.

Sampling

Linked to the section above, the correct sampling technique will also have a strong influence on the validity of the data gathered. If you have chosen a qualitative methodology, did you select non-probability sampling? Was it convenience or purposive or event sampling? How does this impact on the suitability of the data gathered and how will this be reported in the sampling section of your methodology?

Some points to remember in sampling

1. Choose the correct sampling procedure according to methodological approach.

2. Be specific about the sampling technique and make clear reference to it with relevant material to corroborate the choice of sampling method.

3. Articulate how the sampling method will be conducted and how this will impact on the potential research participants.

Chapter 3 provides an outline of a number of sampling techniques which are utilised widely by students at undergraduate and postgraduate levels. The overview shows how the various techniques are incorporated into the research design in a pragmatic fashion.

Data analysis

The analysis process can often be quite daunting for the novice researcher and students are sometimes left feeling adrift in the multitude of data analysis frameworks that are available to them. It may also be difficult to specify how and why a data analysis technique has been chosen and why it is most fitting for the data collected.

The gathering and subsequent analysis of qualitative data can often be perceived as a less onerous and more easily managed option for analysis in comparison with quantitative analysis. However, qualitative data analysis is as involved and complex as quantitative analysis and is a lengthy and detailed process. Early career researchers also often remark that whilst there is a plethora of literature on the theory of qualitative analysis and the conceptual underpinning of the work, it is quite difficult to locate a 'how to' guide in relation to the various stages of thematic analysis for exploratory qualitative research (which is largely what students utilise in their first forays into qualitative research methods and analysis). An example of a straightforward and easy to access guide is offered by Philip Burnard (1991); he presents a framework for thematic analysis and a step-by-step pathway to the process of conducting qualitative data analysis with interview transcripts.

Chapter 5 focuses on the analysis of qualitative data in audit and research evaluation projects derived from interviews and focus groups. The focus is basic thematic analysis which underpins a number of methods of qualitative data analysis.

Quantitative data analysis requires a set of skills which are not necessarily premised on mathematical prowess but rather on the use of logic and pragmatism. The majority of candidates who use quantitative methods for undergraduate or postgraduate projects learn to use a statistical package (most commonly SPSS) and produce a series of graphs and tables to provide a visual representation of the data alongside statistical tests which consider association between variables and, in some cases, the differences in values/scores (see Chapter 6).

Chapter 7 considers a basic level of quantitative data analysis which uses the SPSS package to house and analyse the data. The chapter includes a discussion on the production of charts and graphs, measures of central tendency and dispersion, tests for association and tests of mean scores most commonly used in small-scale research reports.

Reporting of findings

Findings must be reported in a legible and concise format and be contextualised within a logical and coherent structure. The reader should be able to follow a clear sequencing of findings and to locate a certain theme or subheading within the results easily, without having to wade through swathes of irrelevant text or description. On occasions, some student researchers may veer off on specific tangents and lose sight of the objectives. Whilst it is expected that a number of findings may arise that were not originally intended, it is good practice to make sure you have addressed your intended research objectives via the first draft of the findings. You may then incorporate the additional results that have been highlighted as a corollary of the research process.

Some points to remember in the reporting of findings

1. It is a good idea to reiterate the objectives at the beginning of the findings section to remind yourself and the reader of the primary purpose of the research.

2. Do not report the findings incrementally according to *each* question in the survey, focus group or semi-structured interview schedule but instead try to follow the initial structure outlined within your aims and objectives at the beginning of the project.

3. Try to avoid the discussion of other project findings within your results section and maintain a focus on a clear synopsis of the findings from your project.

4. Clearly label figures and tables in the findings section and keep heading fonts consistent throughout the text.

5. Do not insert tables/figures without supportive discussion as this engenders a disjointed presentation without clarity and explanation.

6. In reporting quantitative findings highlight percentages followed by numbers 20% (n = 132) and follow the guidelines in statistical manuals for the reporting of results from statistical tests (for example, see Pallant, 2013).

7. In the reporting of qualitative data, remember to italicise the direct quotations, indent and provide a code for each excerpt.

Contextualising the findings

The findings should be set within a firm literary and evidence-based framework which will provide an analytical discussion of some of the key points in the findings section. Select a number of key points from the findings section and make note of them in a separate file. Consult research and extant literature from your literature review section and any additional relevant material that you may have gathered in the interim. Subsequently, read your findings again in the light of the literature that you have gathered and make notes as to whether any of your findings are substantiated or refuted by the key literature points. Next, try to contextualise your findings with those from the literature review and do try to provide a reflective analysis of the points made. Begin by describing one key finding and then discuss similar findings from one or possibly two other studies (see below). Repeat the process until you have created a strong thematic framework in which your key findings are presented within an analytical discussion.

Some points to remember in contextualising the findings

1. Use up-to-date sources to showcase your findings in a corroborative and relevant knowledge base. Choose findings from research projects which are no more than ten years old. However, other literary sources such as key texts or historical legislative/policy documents may be drawn from older sources.

2. As outlined in other sections, plan the structure of this chapter in advance and prepare to write with a clear idea of how you wish to proceed without meandering too much from the points you are trying to make.

Chapter 9 guides the reader in a consideration of the *discussion* and *conclusions* sections of their report or oral presentation. There is a helpful guide of how to extrapolate the primary findings and also how to outline the limitations of the study. There are also some very useful tips about how to link the study findings to contextual factors such as law, policy, standards and service development strategies.

Presenting the report

The presentation of the report is crucial to how the findings and discussion (and indeed all the components of the report) are viewed. The reader does not think about the author's agonising months of trawling through literature, formulating interview or survey questions, conducting the field work, transcribing, inputting, analysing and writing up. They are concerned only with the research product and are expecting an articulate read with concise points of summary and conclusion.

The content will speak for itself but it must be dressed within a reader-friendly format with a coherent structure that will induce the reader to peruse the project fully and with enthusiasm.

Some points to remember in presenting the report

1. Use a clear title page with an appropriate font.

2. Use contents pages and include all headings and subheadings.

3. Show a list of tables and figures in the contents pages as they are presented in the report.

4. Maintain the same font for headings and subheadings throughout the report.

5. Use Harvard referencing in the report and check your institution guidelines for more detailed advice.

6. Include supplementary tables in the appendices.

7. Include ethical approval documents, project information sheets and informed consent documents in the appendices.

See **Chapter 8** for further guidelines on the presentation of findings in the research project.

Publication and dissemination

Over the last number of years, we have had the enjoyable experience of supervising master's and PhD students to completion and throughout that period have learned some valuable lessons about the many and varied small mistakes that can be made. However, we are always pleasantly surprised as regards the creative and wonderfully lateral approaches to research that are used by a high number of enthusiastic researchers. It is then with great pleasure that we see many inexperienced researchers complete an empirical research project and reach the publication and dissemination stages. There have also been a range of examples where a number of the projects have been awarded prizes, or indeed have influenced practice or had an impact on policy at a regional level. In addition, a number of master's level projects have been published by the students in prestigious journals such as *Social Work Education* and the *British Journal of Social Work*.

However, before that stage, the majority of students provide their work to their respective institutions for marking and accreditation. This may also be followed by dissemination to the team if the students are in a practice setting or, for some, by providing the results of the study to the project participants. A formal presentation process may be part of some courses' marking arrangements or students may choose to present the findings at the request of the team managers, other social workers, other students or service users.

Some points to remember in publication and dissemination

1. If you are required to make a presentation, ensure that you present to your workplace audience or fellow students who have an interest in the subject area and/or research.

2. Prepare the presentation with plenty of time to spare prior to the date of presentation.

3. Ensure that you practise over one or two days prior to presenting and time the presentation.

4. If moving quite quickly to dissemination to other agencies or interested parties, publish the work in a more commercial format, funding permitting. Alternatively, for a cheaper option, utilise the reprographic service in your local university or library to get the document bound and fronted with a plastic cover.

5. Try to publish at least one article from your dissertation thesis with the support of your supervisor(s) who will most likely guide you throughout the process and assist with editing, etc.

6. Check 'author guidelines' for a number of journals in your subject area, making note of journal aims and objectives, scope, audience and publication guidelines. Additionally, check out a number of articles, similar to your own in methodology or subject, within one or two journals you have targeted for publication.

The following chapters provide a more detailed overview of how to begin, develop, maintain and complete a research project. We wish you success on your research journey and look forward to reading your work in print!

1: Reviewing the Literature

Chapter aims

This chapter will:

- outline the purpose and scope of a literature review to underpin a research, audit or service evaluation project, and define important terms;
- explain the main steps of a literature review, namely:
    - defining a clear question;
    - identifying relevant studies;
    - appraising research quality;
    - synthesising studies.
- consider systematic *reviews*;
- explore the characteristics that make literature reviews robust, publishable and useful as evidence to inform practice and policy.

Definition and purpose of a literature review

A 'literature review' aims to give a balanced overview of current knowledge on a particular research question, including the substantive content of research studies and an appraisal of their quality. In the present context, the essential purpose of a literature review is to ensure that the proposed project – whether research, audit or service evaluation – is building on what is already known. If doing the project can be compared to joining an international academic conversation, then the literature review is listening to what people have already been saying before speaking (Grinnell and Unrau, 2011). Duplicating work that has already answered a question satisfactorily is regarded as unethical, placing a pointless burden on participants and researchers, and wasting public or charitable funding. There may, of course, be a valid purpose in replicating a study in a different legal, organisational or cultural environment, but that would be answering a different question such as about generalisability or applicability in a different context.

There is normally far more published research on a topic than most people know about, and discovering this is one of the joys of reviewing the literature. Of course, it may be justifiable to carry out similar research to a previous study in order to establish results more robustly or to demonstrate applicability in a different cultural or organisational context. But in that case it is still important to know the detail of the previous study so as to learn from the methodology and to ensure that the methods and results from your study can be compared with previous ones. The literature review also helps to consolidate your understanding of the main theoretical concepts used in the topic area.

Reading for your research, audit or evaluation project is likely to include:

- introductory contextual material to locate the *topic* and explain its importance and relationship to social work such as definition of terms, prevalence or incidence of social problems, description of current services, social welfare statutes, case law and national policies, standards of practice and regulations, guidance, policies and procedures;

- books and articles providing theoretical material related to your *topic*;

- textbooks on detailed aspects of *research methods*; and

- journal articles publishing the original results of empirical research on your proposed *research question*, i.e. the particular aspect of your topic that you are studying.

Our focus here is on the last of these – published research on your specific question – which we will refer to as the *literature review*. However, the general principles, knowledge and skills that are discussed here will be relevant to other types of literature searches too.

In writing a report on your study it is important that you are clear on the different types of literature, and it may be helpful to use the bullet list above as a guide to structuring your writing. Material relating to the *context* should do just what the title says: set the general context. The theoretical framework from which you take your perspective on the project tends to follow next, although this is sometimes not clearly delineated in smaller-scale studies. Material on empirical research – what is already known on the topic – logically comes next. We refer to this as the *literature review*, and that is the focus of this chapter. This literature review leads the reader into your research *question* clarifying the knowledge gap that you are addressing. Material on research methods will go in your *methods* section. If your search for publications covering previous research on your topic retrieves articles that are more useful in other sections then of course you can use them there.

The essential steps of a literature review of previous research on a topic are: (1) to have a clear question; (2) to identify relevant literature; (3) to appraise the quality of this literature; and (4) to synthesise the relevant material identified (Taylor et al., 2015). We will discuss these in turn and we will focus primarily on the first two aspects as our experience suggests that this will be more useful to most readers of this book.

How much rigour you apply to each stage of your literature review depends on the purpose of the literature review and on the time and resources available. You must create a manageable process, and clear decision making is required. In discussion with your supervisor or research team, you need to manage the breadth of the topic and the rigour to be applied to each stage of the literature review process. You should record these decisions and the rationale. One might expect to see increasing rigour being used along a continuum from a qualifying (Bachelor's degree) course to a post-qualifying (taught master's) course to a PhD or a research grant application, and up to that required as a basis for professional guidance or for a *systematic review* acceptable to the Cochrane or Campbell collaborations (see below). Literature reviews may be assessed as part of post-qualifying education and training (Taylor et al., 2010) and are a valuable form of knowledge in their own right. Our focus in this book is on the academic level required for master's or final-year undergraduate programmes, and for professional post-qualifying schemes.

Defining your review question

Specifying a precise question for a literature review is a very similar task to specifying a precise question for a research, audit or service evaluation project. Generally, both will address the same question as you will wish to ascertain what is already known on your question before commencing empirical work. How tightly you define the topic may depend on how much published literature there is in the field. You want to create a manageable process within your time and resources, and must manage the breadth of the topic as an aspect of that.

Identifying relevant research – an introduction

Having defined a clear question, the next stage of the literature review is to identify relevant research using an appropriately robust process. In general, this will involve searching web-based bibliographic databases supplemented by hand-searching. We will also discuss the use of mechanisms to search the internet. Traditionally, research degrees required a literature review to be completed prior to the empirical work. However, in the past they were rarely based on any explicit methodology. There was much scope for bias, whether intentional or unintentional. The theoretical orientation, academic community, and national context of the research student and supervisor could influence the scope of literature included, and this might not have been recognised or acknowledged. Increasingly, explicit methodologies are now being used for searching for relevant research (Taylor et al., 2003; Taylor et al., 2007; McFadden et al., 2012), as well as for other aspects of literature reviewing. The development of web-based bibliographic databases that contain abstracts of journal articles has transformed methods of identifying relevant research.

Selecting bibliographic databases

There is no one major database that one might regard as a primary source for identifying social work research, perhaps because it is such an eclectic discipline. So, a number of databases are normally used. The databases available for searching are steadily evolving in terms of their scope and facilities. All universities and some social work employers subscribe to a range of these databases. Sometimes several databases are provided by the publishers on a common platform, such as OVIDSP, *Proquest* or *Web of Knowledge*. Increasingly, a search option is provided so that you can search several databases simultaneously. However, this has limited usefulness for rigorous searching as the platform is attempting to search across databases that have different indexing systems (see Table 1.1) using a standard search. For high-quality searching on such database platforms, you need to ensure that you search each database separately. Publishers of journals are increasingly providing systems for searching the range of journals that they publish. As publications of interest to social work come from a range of publishers we do not consider these explicitly here, although the principles of searching should still apply. Some examples of relevant databases are given in Table 1.1. For further discussion about the quality of databases, see Taylor (2009).

Table 1.1 Databases that might be useful to identify social work research articles

Database title	Description
SCOPUS	A huge bibliographic database with over 49 million records, abstracted from over 20,000 journals across all academic subject areas. With such a diverse database it is particularly important to consider whether people outside your field will attribute diverse meanings to your search terms.
Medline	A very large, international database published by the US National Library of Medicine. It contains over 19 million records abstracted from over 5,500 journals including high-quality social work journals. It is good for social work topics that interface with medicine (e.g. child protection, mental health, elder care) but less useful for a topic on criminal justice or community development. On the OVID platform it is one of the highest quality databases from a user perspective.
PsycInfo	A large, international database published by the American Psychological Association. It contains over three million records from 2,500 journals including many of relevance to social work, particularly where we are interested in experimental studies that might provide evidence to underpin practice or papers on psychosocial constructs such as 'self-esteem', 'stress' or 'resilience'. On the OVID platform it is one of the highest quality databases from a user perspective.

Database title	Description
Cumulative Index to Nursing and Allied Health Literature (CINAHL)	A large, international database of nearly three million records that abstracts from about 3,000 journals including many of interest to social work. As with *Medline*, it is good for topics that interface with health care. Disability topics may be found more easily by searching for particular conditions.
Social Science Citation Index (SSCI)	A large, international database for the social sciences covering about 2,500 journals. It has a 'citation searching' feature which enables you to access readily the references within an article that you retrieve if they are also on the database. However, you should note that it has no indexing system (see below) which limits its ease of use for thorough searching on a topic.
Applied Social Sciences Index and Abstracts (ASSIA)	This contains nearly 400,000 records abstracted from 500 journals covering the range of social sciences.
Health Management Information Consortium (HMIC)	A UK database abstracting journals on health and social care management. It contains about 300,000 records.
Social Care Online	The national database provided by the Social Care Institute for Excellence, a UK government-sponsored organisation, as part of its mission to improve social care services by disseminating knowledge. It covers nearly 700 journals related to social care (including social work) and contains about 200,000 records.
Social Services Abstracts (SSA)	A US-based database that contains about 200,000 records, abstracting from about 1,300 journals in the field of social work, human services, social welfare, social policy and community development.
Social Work Abstracts (SWA)	Published by the National Association of Social Workers in the USA, and is frequently unavailable in UK universities. It contains about 75,000 records and covers about 500 journals relevant to social work.
Criminal Justice Abstracts	Includes over 200,000 records from the most relevant sources for criminal justice.
National Criminal Justice Reference Service Abstracts	Contains over 200,000 records related to criminal justice, including juvenile justice and drug control.
Nexis UK	Covers legislation and case law for Europe, including the UK, and contains over 20,000 records.

'Grey' literature

One question that you will need to address at an early stage is whether or not to include 'grey literature'. This is a term that is used to apply to any publication that is not peer reviewed by reviewers with expertise in the field and includes conference papers, organisation reports and theses and dissertations produced as part of academic studies. In favour of excluding grey literature is the argument that the highest quality research will be published in peer-reviewed journals, if only because it is in generally the interests of researchers to do this. There is enough of a challenge in sifting through the vast amount of mediocre quality research in social work, anyway! In favour of including grey literature is the argument that there may be commercial or political pressures not to publish material more widely, particularly if the study produced results that might be embarrassing to established political or organisational interests or shows that an intervention is not effective. If you do decide to include grey literature you will need to show how you intend to search thoroughly for this as it is not generally included in the major databases listed above. SIGLE is a database which specialises in abstracting some types of grey literature.

Constructing a search formula

The guiding principle for developing a search for bibliographic databases is that you want to retrieve as many relevant items as possible whilst avoiding as far as possible retrieving irrelevant items (Taylor, 2003). For this purpose, your search question must be translated into clear concepts. Essentially, the concepts reflect the main aspects of your topic. The first task is to identify the main concepts within the question and to give these a name for your own convenience.

Example – Identifying concept groups

QUESTION: What causes older people to fall within residential or nursing homes?

CONCEPT GROUPS: ‹older people› AND ‹falls› AND ‹institutional care›

QUESTION: How often are social workers assaulted at work?

CONCEPT GROUPS: ‹social worker› AND ‹violence›

QUESTION: What effect does disclosure of childhood sexual abuse have on the family?

CONCEPT GROUPS: ‹disclose› AND ‹sexual abuse› AND ‹family›

The essential point is that we are interested only in articles that contain all of the concepts that we have identified. Thus in the first example, we are not interested in other aspects of older people in institutional care – such as nutrition or care regimes, for example – but only in falls. Sometimes the identification of concepts might seem ambiguous. In the example above, the search concepts would be equally valid to retrieve articles on violence *by* social workers (if there are any!) as to violence *to* social workers. It is not realistic to put the concept of 'to' or 'by' into a database search and spurious articles will have to be rejected by hand from the hits retrieved. It is important to note that the concepts that you are defining are those that are most appropriate for your particular purpose. For example, there are differences between residential homes and nursing homes in terms of admission criteria, registration requirements, staffing, etc. However, it may be that for your purpose – an interest in older people falling in such settings due to the flooring used – they form one homogeneous concept of institutional care.

There are some concepts which are unable to be expressed effectively in the search formula. Concepts such as 'effects of', 'effectiveness of', 'prevalence of' and 'incidence of' are frequently omitted for this reason, and also because such terms are often omitted from article titles. Concepts such as 'experiences of' or 'perceptions of' are also often omitted, although an illustration below gives an approach to including these. Typically, two to four concepts are required to express database searches on social work topics. If you are searching for studies of the effectiveness of an intervention, a common acronym in health and social care for structuring a search is 'PICO': Population, Intervention, Comparison and Outcome (Centre for Reviews and Dissemination, 2009).

Example – PICO structure for a search on effectiveness of an intervention

QUESTION: Is reality orientation more effective than social contact for helping older people with dementia not to exhibit problematic behaviours?

- Population: people over 65 years with dementia

- Intervention: validation therapy (reality orientation)

- Comparison intervention: social contact

- Outcome measure: behaviour

The concepts that you have identified are combined by using the operator 'AND' (derived from Boolean algebra) when you put these into a database search. This is a way of expressing algebraically that we require all of the concepts to be present for the abstract of that article to be retrieved by the search as a 'hit'. The way that you express this operator varies between databases; in this text we will use capitalised AND to indicate that it is a database operator that carries out a specific function in combining concepts in this way. Every database has a 'help' function which will tell you what symbols to use for the various techniques outlined in this chapter.

Most of the databases have an index system such that each abstract added is indexed against the standard set of terms adopted by that database. Indexing is time-consuming and skilled work! You will probably find that most, but not all, of your concepts are captured reasonably by the index terms on the database. If index terms are available on the database, then you can use those to express the relevant concept in your search. If your search involves a concept that does not correspond reasonably to an index term on a particular database, then you must use 'text-term searching', i.e. searching in the titles and abstracts for specific words that you identify.

If there is no index term corresponding to your concept and you have to use text-term searching, then you will need to identify the possible alternative words that might be used by an author of an article to express that concept. It is important that you do not think only of your own preferred term or what is regarded as acceptable in your society. Terms vary over time and across countries and cultures; your task is to retrieve relevant articles on the chosen topic. In particular you need to be aware of terminology that is unique to your culture or jurisdiction, or relatively so. For example, 'looked after children' is a term used only (as far as I am aware) in the UK. Authors in most countries would understand better a term such as 'children in state care' and are more likely to use something like this.

Example – Alternative terms for text-term searching

CONCEPT: learning disability

ALTERNATIVE TERMS: mental handicap, mental disorder, learning difficulty, intellectual impairment, intellectual disability.

In order to express these alternative terms for a concept we use the Boolean algebra operator 'OR'. This is used to link words or terms within a concept group. It means in effect that we do not mind which of these words are used to represent that concept. An article (in its title or abstract) may contain any of these terms (or more than one of them) for it to be acceptable in relation to that particular concept. The way that you express this operator varies between databases; in this text we will use capitalised OR to indicate that it is a database operator that carries out a specific function in combining equivalent terms within concepts in this way. This is illustrated in the following example.

Example – Combining terms within a concept using 'OR'

For example:

patient OR client OR service user;

youth OR adolescent OR teenager;

'restorative practice' OR 'youth conferencing' OR 'family group conferencing'.

The crucial issue, then, is how we combine the use of 'AND' and 'OR' within an effective search. For our last and most important acknowledgement of Boolean algebra I need to remind you of what you learned in school about the use of brackets within an equation, although we are using words not numbers. What is in the brackets must be treated as a meaningful entity in itself ('do what is in the brackets first') before combining this with what is outside the brackets. We put terms expressing a particular concept linked by 'OR' within brackets. Each concept is within its own brackets and we join the concepts (sets of brackets) with 'AND'. It is easier to understand with an example.

Example – Combining concepts using brackets

For example: (hospital) AND (admission) AND (older people OR elderly OR senior citizens)

When you are combining the terms within a database search it will be useful if you can remember this basic tenet from algebra of ensuring that what is in the brackets is 'addressed first', i.e. is meaningful in itself. Within each bracket you can include as many equivalent terms as you think necessary to capture that particular concept. Note that it does not matter for the resulting search what order is used for concept groups or for terms within concept groups. What is essential is that equivalent terms (for our purpose) are within brackets connected by OR, and that concept groups themselves are joined by AND. On some databases – such as those on the OVID platform – you enter terms in successive rows, and then combine them. On some databases you enter the string of terms joined by the operators: AND, OR and brackets () using the above logic. An example to illustrate the importance of the brackets is given below.

Example – Using brackets and terms correctly and incorrectly

- (older people) AND (Alzheimer's OR dementia)

IS NOT THE SAME AS

- (older people AND Alzheimer's) OR (dementia)

The first search is meaningful and useful. We are interested in articles that refer to dementia or to Alzheimer's in relation to older people. The second search will retrieve articles on Alzheimer's in relation to older people, and articles on dementia with any age group. There is no sound logic to this second version.

Text-term searching

You have perhaps been wondering what to do about different parts of speech, word endings and variant spellings. A computer will only retrieve what it is told to retrieve, and of course cannot 'understand' that 'adolescent' has anything to do with 'adolescence' or that 'teach' is connected etymologically with 'taught'. Most databases have a system for truncation and wild cards to simplify this aspect, such as in the examples below. This enables the user to represent a number of alternative letters with a symbol - usually an asterisk (*), but sometimes a question mark (?) or a dollar sign ($).

Example – Using truncation and wild cards

*disab** WILL RETRIEVE: *disabled, disablement, disability, disabilities*

*social work** WILL RETRIEVE: *social work, social worker, social workers*

*counsel** WILL RETRIEVE: *counsellor, counselor, counsellors, counselors, counselling*

*teach** WILL RETRIEVE: *teacher, teachers, teaching* (BUT NOT *taught* !!!)

*organi*ation* WILL RETRIEVE: *organisation, organization*

You will have noticed in some of the above examples that quotation/speech marks have been used. These are to mark out phrases. If the words of a phrase are put in to the search without speech marks then you are likely to retrieve more irrelevant items. Their use makes the search more precise (see below). Note that on some databases truncation and wild cards can be used within speech marks for phrases, whereas on others they cannot.

Abbreviations

Abbreviations are in common use for some concepts and organisations. It is recommended in this case that you use both the abbreviated and the full version, joined by 'OR' within the brackets for that concept group of course. For example:

- ASD OR autism spectrum disorder;
- CVA OR cardio vascular accident OR stroke;
- HRA OR Human Rights Act;
- LAC OR looked after children;
- UNESCO OR United Nations Educational, Scientific and Cultural Organisation;
- WHO OR World Health Organisation.

Process of constructing the search

You will find that some of your concepts are expressed by index terms on a database whilst others are not. Databases tend to update their index terms once a year, to keep abreast of developments in knowledge. However, you will recognise that there is a balance; if the index terms are changed too often users will feel lost when they are searching. As mentioned above, it does not matter in what order you enter the concepts into the database in terms of the final search outcome. However, for the purposes of developing your search I would advise that you enter first the best established concepts, i.e. those that are most likely to have index terms, and work towards the least clearly defined concepts. Checking on the hits retrieved as you go along will give you some idea of whether you are on the right track. You may find that on some databases the index terms available enable you to combine two of your concepts whereas on other databases they do not (see Example – Combining concepts on a database).

Example – Combining concepts on a database

QUESTION: Is cognitive behavioural therapy effective for improving family relationships?

CONCEPTS: (CBT) AND (family) AND (relationship*)

OPERATIONALISING on Medline using index terms you only need two concept groups for a reasonable basic search:

(CBT) AND (family relationship* OR family conflict*)

NB: Note use of two Medical Subject Headings (MeSH) index terms to express the second concept.

Hand searching

Although the main focus of our searching is web-based bibliographic databases, you need to recognise that even the most thorough searching of databases will miss some of the relevant literature. Therefore, you might supplement database searching with *hand searching*. This is the term used for looking at the references within relevant articles that you have found, contacting eminent authors in the field and carrying out other similar activities to build on the database search. Even if the database searching retrieves only a half of the relevant articles available, it is still much more thorough and less biased than relying only on hand searching approaches.

Quality of database searching

The quality of your search can be considered along two dimensions: *sensitivity* and *precision*. *Sensitivity* is the fraction of the total available articles that are retrieved by a search on a particular database. *Precision* is the ability of a search to exclude irrelevant items. This topic is beyond the scope of this volume; the interested reader is referred to Taylor (2003) and McFadden et al. (2012).

Search filters and strings

The better databases provide mechanisms to filter the hits so as to improve precision of searching. Some provide a filter for 'research' which is useful to separate empirical papers from theoretical and ideological papers, and other material in journals such as editorials which also may be abstracted. Some, such as Medline, have filters for stages of studies (trials) of effectiveness of interventions. The search strings illustrated are useful to add as an additional concept group at the end of your search where filters are not available to refine the search (Fisher et al., 2006). Some examples of search strings for qualitative research and for studies of effectiveness are given below.

> ### Example – Search strings for research methods
>
> QUALITATIVE STUDIES: (attitude* OR experience* OR opinion* OR perception* OR perspectives* OR satisf* OR view*)
>
> STUDIES OF EFFECTIVENESS: (effect* OR impact* OR outcome* OR 'treatment outcome')

The database may also have a filter to allow you to limit the number of years back to search. The default will be to search back as far as the database records. This varies greatly. Most databases commenced operation some time around the middle 1980s. However, Medline includes records back to 1946 and PsycInfo back to 1806! In terms of your final search, this facility is helpful in prompting you to consider the date range for your literature review. Do you want it to be 'up to the present' or does it make more sense to cut off at the end of the last calendar year? Do you want to go as far back on each particular database as it will allow (i.e. a different date range on each database) or does it make more sense for this particular literature review to have a defined earliest publication date? Another use for the date filters is while you are developing your search. Reducing the numbers of years searched will mean that each search takes a few milliseconds less. Whilst you are experimenting with new search terms and looking at the hits to see how relevant they are this may be useful, for example, by limiting the search to just the past five years. You can then set whatever date range you decide when you run the final search.

Once you have achieved a search formula with which you are content, there are various options for managing the results of your search. Typically, you can email the results to yourself from the database as well being able to download them into software for managing references such as RefMan. If you are doing your searches to retrieve the most recent publications possible, then it is suggested that you run all the finalised searches on one day so as to have equitable coverage across databases.

Availability of articles

These databases that we are considering focus on including abstracts of articles. The abstract should be enough to determine whether that article is relevant for your review although, sadly, the quality of some abstracts leaves much to be desired. If you are unsure about whether an article is relevant you will have to look at the full text, for which you will need to use whatever system is available in the university. Normally, journal articles are also available electronically.

Searching the internet

Increasingly, there are facilities for identifying journal articles through the internet itself, by using web search engines such as *GoogleScholar*, *dogpile*, *Ask*, etc. Use of web search engines is hindered by the fact that the user cannot ascertain the commercial search algorithms used and, thus, has limited control of the search process. However, there is increasing interest in this subject, and there are likely to be developments in this area (Bergman, 2012; McFadden et al., 2012).

> ### Example – A rigorous search using a database and a web search engine
>
> *Medline*: ('adult protection' OR 'elder abuse' OR 'elder mistreatment' OR 'vulnerable adult' OR 'elder neglect') AND (decision* OR judg*ment OR factor* OR indicator*)
>
> *Google Scholar*: ('adult protection' OR 'elder abuse' OR 'elder mistreatment' OR 'vulnerable adult' OR 'elder neglect') AND (decision OR judgement OR judgment OR factor OR indicator)
>
> (Killick and Taylor, 2009)

Appraising the quality of studies

Having identified relevant studies, the next stage of the process is, logically, to appraise the quality of the research retrieved before venturing into a synthesis of the results or findings. For higher-quality literature reviews, such as for determining professional guidelines or systematic reviews for the Cochrane or Campbell collaborations, this is an essential step. However, it is still uncommon for literature reviews undertaken as part of academic studies to include this stage where decisions are made about including or excluding studies on the basis of their quality. Partly this may be because of the work involved, but also perhaps of the complexity and politics of making such decisions. In keeping with the interest of our readership, we will give only a brief overview here and provide references for those who wish to pursue the topic further.

In general, the rigour of the research that you identify for your literature review can be appraised using the tenets of good research as expounded in the other chapters of this book. In particular this might include:

- appropriateness of the method for the research question;

- appropriateness and size of the sample;

- quality of the data collection tool (questionnaire or aide-memoire for interviews or focus groups); and

- appropriateness and rigour of the analysis.

Data on the methods used in each study will need to be extracted in order to undertake this appraisal. This is often achieved most easily by creating a table containing columns for each of the main characteristics on which you want to extract data. This might include: overall design, the data collection tool, and the nature and size of the sample.

Points to note

You will begin to appreciate that with so many aspects to consider, it is not easy to create justifiable rules that can be applied to rate the quality of research. A study that is better in one respect may be weaker in another. One key question might be what effect the weaknesses might have, or whether a study has no substantial weaknesses that would undermine its rigour.

In general terms, there are a number of major approaches to appraising quality using tools that guide the extraction of the most important elements of the study.

1. Tools that seek to appraise quality across every research design. Examples would be the TAPUPA (Transparency, Accuracy, Purpose, Utility, Propriety, Accessibility) framework of the Social Care Institute for Excellence (Pawson et al., 2003), the framework of Joel Fischer (1981) and the tool by Benton and McCormack (2000).

2. Tools that seek to appraise research according to the main categories. The text by Taylor et al. (2015) contains tools for appraising these three main study designs: surveys; qualitative research; and (quasi-)experimental studies. The approach adopted by the UK Cabinet Office in relation to qualitative research (Spencer et al., 2003) falls into this category: an approach spanning all qualitative designs (cf Drisko, 1997).

3. Approaches that claim that each research design and approach can only be appraised according to the tenets of that particular method. Thus ethnographic studies, for example, would only be appraised according to the tenets of ethnography rather than within a broader framework of principles applying to qualitative studies in general or to research in general.

It is valuable to appraise the methods of studies in your literature review not only so as to weigh up their contribution to knowledge on the topic, but also to guide the methods of your own empirical work. It is worthwhile indicating in the *methods* section of your own study how the methods of studies in your literature review have influenced your own methodology.

The above examples give guidance on appraising quality, but rarely include scoring systems that might give explicit criteria on which to determine whether a study should be regarded as 'good enough' to be included in your review. There are various approaches to this task (e.g. Taylor et al., 2007), but the only schema that has widespread recognition is the *hierarchy of evidence* which relates to research designs, not sampling or data collection tools. It must be noted that this is only designed for studies of the effectiveness of interventions, not studies designed to address understandings, perceptions, prevalence, incidence or correlations such as qualitative and surveys are designed to do (Crombie, 2005). The hierarchy of evidence creates a hierarchy of research designs such that, other things being equal, these designs are in rank order in terms of their rigour in avoiding bias and other confounding factors in addressing questions of the effectiveness of planned interventions (Centre for Reviews and Dissemination, 2009). This hierarchy of evidence is now internationally recognised for its intended purpose, for research regardless of topic area where the research question is about the effectiveness of a planned intervention. There is no widely accepted schema for research on other questions.

One criterion that you can use for the literature review part of your contextual material is to include only empirical studies, and exclude from this section those that are theoretical or ideological.

Synthesising studies

Having identified relevant research and decided which relevant studies to include in terms of quality, the next stage is to synthesise the results or findings of included studies. The traditional approach of creating a coherent narrative that links the studies together is now generally termed a *narrative review.*

A *narrative review* might be structured according to the major themes or topics within the literature. Another alternative is to take a chronological approach, demonstrating the development of ideas over time.

If there are a number of quantitative studies using a similar design, a *meta-analysis* can be undertaken to combine the results of the studies. 'The term *meta-analysis*, has come to encompass all of the methods and techniques of quantitative research synthesis…' (Lipsey and Wilson, 2001, p1). Studies that are conceptually comparable and use comparable research designs may be combined in a meta-analysis in order to draw the most robust conclusions across the studies. Studies are summarised primarily by viewing the results in terms of the effect size reported. Meta-analysis involves tabulating the strength and direction of each statistical relationship in the included studies (Cooper, 1998).

If there are a number of qualitative studies which gather data using interviews or focus groups, a *meta-synthesis* can be undertaken to combine the findings of the studies. *Qualitative meta-synthesis* is an 'interpretive integration of qualitative findings in primary research reports that are in the form of interpretive syntheses of data: ether conceptual-thematic descriptions or interpretive explanations' (Sandelowski and Barroso, 2007, p199). This adds additional rigour by comparison with narrative review. The focus of *meta-synthesis* is to represent accurately the constructs of the studies and synthesising the findings by thematic groupings (Spencer et al., 2003). One challenge is to try not to lose the appeal of the figures of speech, metaphors and written representations of reality in the original studies. A key issue is that the typical journal paper reporting qualitative research often contains too little original data to enable meta-synthesis.

It is also possible to focus on synthesising only studies that use the same qualitative research approach, e.g. synthesising ethnographic studies through meta-ethnography (Noblit and Hare, 1988). This has the potential to be a more robust approach within a narrowly defined topic of study. However, in an applied area of study such as social work we are more likely to want to synthesise across a variety of approaches to derive the core findings to inform practice.

As with other steps of literature reviewing, a robust synthesis of literature employs a structure that is transparent and open to scrutiny. A methodological approach to synthesis has the additional benefit that the findings are subject to deeper scrutiny than in the traditional narrative review. It is possible of course within a larger project to undertake more than one synthesis of data, perhaps a *meta-analysis* of a more limited number of studies together with a narrative review of all studies.

Systematic reviews and use of reviews

The term *systematic review* is used to describe a literature review that has an explicit and robust methodology for each stage described above: (1) identifying relevant studies; (2) appraising study quality; and (3) synthesising findings of relevant papers (Coren and Fisher, 2006; Dempster, 2003; Petticrew and Roberts, 2006). Increasingly the term *systematic narrative review* is being used for literature reviews that have an explicit process of literature searching (with or without an explicit quality appraisal) combined with a narrative synthesis (Killick and Taylor, 2009).

From PhD level upwards a literature review should be publishable as a journal article in its own right, although this depends essentially on the degree of methodological rigour used in the process. It is also possible to publish original work on an aspect of the methodology of rigorous literature reviewing.

The most rigorous literature reviews are the *systematic reviews* (Chalmers and Altman, 1995) of the effectiveness of interventions carried out as part of the Cochrane collaboration (focusing on health and social care interventions) or the Campbell collaboration (focusing on criminal justice, educational, social welfare and international development interventions). The Cochrane Library includes systematic reviews of over 70 interventions that might be carried out by social workers (some requiring post-qualifying training), and there a number relevant to our profession in the Campbell Library also.

Activity

- Define a question related to practice that could be addressed by research.
- Structure a search on this question in terms of concept groups.
- Identify variant terms to use for each concept.
- Use this search on an appropriate database such as PsycInfo or Medline.

Summary

- The main stages of a literature review are:

    o identifying relevant studies;
    o appraising research quality; and
    o synthesising relevant quality studies.

- Defining a clear, meaningful and 'answerable' question is essential, and will usually be an iterative process developing the question as available studies are related to the needs of the service.
- Learning how to construct a search formula on bibliographic databases is an essential skill if a reasonably comprehensive search on a topic is to be achieved.
- An introduction has been given to the principles of appraising research quality, pointing the reader towards more detailed resources for this purpose (Taylor et al., 2015).
- The main types of synthesis have been identified and outlined as: meta-analysis of quantitative data; meta-synthesis of qualitative data; and narrative synthesis of the conclusions of studies across study designs.
- Systematic reviews – reviews that have an explicit and robust methodology for all three stages: study identification; quality appraisal; and synthesis – have been described, together with pointers to the major international initiatives in systematic reviewing of studies of the effectiveness of social work interventions.
- The term 'systematic narrative review' is used increasingly for studies that have a methodology for study identification (and sometimes also for quality appraisal) followed by a narrative synthesis.

Further reading

Campbell Collaboration (C2) www.campbellcollaboration.org – an international non-profit and independent organisation dedicated to making available up-to-date, accurate information on the effectiveness of social, behavioural, educational and criminal justice interventions.

Cochrane Collaboration (CC) www.cochrane.org – an international non-profit and independent organisation, dedicated to making up-to-date, accurate information about the effectiveness of health and social care interventions readily available worldwide.

Social Care Institute for Excellence (SCIE) www.scie.org.uk – improves the lives of people who use care services by sharing knowledge about what works, in particular by providing an online database (Social Care Online), commissioning systematic reviews, and producing resources that summarise key messages for good practice.

Taylor, BJ, Killick, C and McGlade, A (2015) *Understanding and Using Research in Social Work*. London: Sage.

This clearly-written textbook contains separate chapters on the main stages of reviewing the literature – identifying relevant studies; appraising research quality; and synthesis – as well as chapters on the translation of research into practice by individual professionals and organisations.

2: Selecting Your Research Method

Chapter aims

This chapter will:

- guide you in selecting the appropriate method for your research, professional audit or service evaluation project;
- clarify types of study question, including:
  - o questions of the effectiveness of a planned intervention;
  - o the perspectives of service recipients or service providers;
  - o prevalence or incidence of some aspect of social care services.
- explore the strengths and appropriateness of different research designs for these different questions, including experimental, qualitative, survey and mixed methods;
- discuss the complementary nature of inductive and deductive research, the involvement of the public or service users within studies, and the place of various types of study within the overall enterprise of creating knowledge to develop the practice of the profession;
- illustrate key aspects using examples from social work research.

Types of question

The primary issue in selecting a study design is the type of question being asked rather than the topic under consideration. Almost any design can be used in any topic area, subject to practicalities; the main issue is the question being asked within the topic. The main types of questions that we consider here are about: (1) whether interventions are effective; (2) the perceptions of people receiving or providing services; and (3) gathering information on people's attributes, behaviour, events, beliefs, knowledge of facts, attitudes or opinions to ascertain the prevalence or incidence or whether there are patterns of association between variables. These correspond, respectively, to experimental (and quasi-experimental), qualitative and survey methods. We also consider (4) how to gain a more rounded evaluation of services using a simultaneous mixed-methods approach.

Questions of effectiveness

As a profession that seeks to help people to change (to overcome problems or to improve or maintain some aspect of quality of life) perhaps the main questions we should be asking are about the effectiveness of our social care (including social work) interventions. Having some understanding of what is an appropriate intervention for a presenting client need is central to social work. If our interventions are not effective then we are wasting our clients' and our own time and energy, and deluding society and ourselves. Is family group conferencing effective? Which type of counselling approach is more effective: cognitive behavioural therapy or non-directive counselling or solution-focused brief therapy? Of course, we need to narrow that sort of question down to a particular problem area such as alcohol addiction, depression or post-traumatic stress. Depending on the current extent of knowledge, we would perhaps want to refine the question further by asking about effectiveness in relation to mild rather than severe depression. Questions about the effects (effectiveness) of planned interventions are addressed most robustly using some form of experimental or quasi-experimental study. An example is given below. Experimental and quasi-experimental studies are discussed further in Chapter 6.

Research summary

Randomised controlled intervention design

Objective: To evaluate the effectiveness of cognitive therapy for post-traumatic stress disorder related to terrorism and other civil conflict in Northern Ireland.

Design: Randomised controlled trial.

Setting: Community treatment centre, Northern Ireland.

Participants: 58 consecutive clients with chronic post-traumatic stress disorder (median 5.2 years, range three months to 32 years) mostly resulting from multiple traumas linked to terrorism and other civil conflict.

Interventions: Immediate cognitive therapy when compared with those on the waiting list as the control condition for 12 weeks followed by treatment. Treatment comprised a mean of 5.9 sessions during 12 weeks and 2.0 sessions thereafter.

Main outcome measures: Primary outcome measures were clients' scores for post-traumatic stress disorder (post-traumatic stress diagnostic scale) and depression (Beck Depression Inventory). The secondary outcome measure was scores for occupational and social functioning (work related disability, social disability and family related disability) on the Sheehan Disability Scale.

Results: At 12 weeks after randomisation, immediate cognitive therapy was associated with significantly greater improvement than the waiting list control group in the symptoms of post-traumatic stress disorder (mean difference 9.6, 95 per cent confidence interval 3.6 to 15.6), depression (mean difference 10.1, 4.8 to 15.3), and self-reported occupational and social functioning (mean difference 1.3, 0.3 to 2.5). Effect sizes from before to after treatment were large: post-traumatic stress disorder 1.25, depression 1.05, and occupational and social functioning 1.17. No change was observed in the control group.

Conclusion: Cognitive therapy is an effective treatment for post-traumatic stress disorder related to terrorism and other civil conflict.

(Duffy et al., 2007, p1147)

Questions of perceptions and experiences

Another important question for a service profession is about the perceptions that our clients have of their needs and their experience of services. Their perceptions can most usefully inform how we provide services, even if the question as to which intervention to provide is more effectively addressed by an experimental method as outlined above. Client perceptions and conceptualisation of their needs may provide a greater understanding and empathy with the problems they face. We might also be interested in the perceptions of people providing services, such as foster parents, home care workers and social workers. Their perceptions and conceptualisation of the dynamic of the helping process might provide useful insight into how services are most helpfully provided. Questions about the perceptions and conceptualisation of people about a personal experience, such as a psychosocial need or the receipt or provision of a personal service, are addressed most appropriately using a qualitative approach. An example is given in the research summary below, and qualitative designs are discussed further in Chapters 4 and 5.

Research summary

With the increasing pressure on social and health care resources, professionals have to be more explicit in their decision making regarding the long-term care of older people. This grounded theory study used 19 focus groups and nine semi-structured interviews (99 staff in total) to explore professional perspectives on this decision making. Focus group participants and interviewees comprised care managers, social workers, consultant geriatricians, general medical practitioners, community nurses, home care managers, occupational therapists and hospital discharge support staff. The emerging themes spanned context, clients, families and services. Decisions were often prompted by a crisis, hindering professionals seeking to make a measured assessment. Fear of burglary and assault and the willingness and availability of family to help were viewed as major factors in decisions about living at home. Service availability in terms of public funding for community care, the availability of home care workers and workload pressures on primary care services influenced decision 'thresholds' regarding admission to institutional care. Assessment tools designed to assist decision making about the long-term care of older people need to take into account the critical aspects of individual fears and motivation, family support, and the availability of publicly funded services as well as functional and medical needs.

(Taylor and Donnelly, 2006)

Questions of prevalence and correlation

Thirdly, we may wish to know how common some behaviour or attitudes are within some defined population of people or whether certain factors correlate with others. Examples of prevalence questions are:

- what percentage of people with dementia are living alone?

- what proportion of social workers discuss risk issues with clients at the point of hospital discharge?

- how do people with disabilities rate (compare) the barriers to social inclusion?

- how do the emotional intelligence scores of social workers compare with those of profession X?

- what fraction of the children in state care have mental health problems?

- what proportion of prisoners were abused as children?

Professional audit projects are generally approached using a survey design, as the questions that they are asking focus on prevalence, such as the numbers of people who take specified periods of time in assessment processes, or satisfaction scores (measuring attitudes) of service recipients.

Related to this is that we may wish to know how often some event occurs, such as the incidence of dementia amongst residential and nursing home admissions during the past year or the incidence of suicidal ideation amongst young people looked after by the state, or how often aggressive and violent incidents occur in children's homes. Such questions are also amenable to a survey design, often using secondary data sources such as services records.

Survey designs are most appropriate for questions about the prevalence of personal attributes, attitudes, behaviour and beliefs, etc., incidence of events, and whether there is any pattern of association between such variables. An example is given below. Surveys are discussed further in Chapter 6.

Research summary

In order to understand better the needs of clients and to inform the delivery of services, referrals to the North Belfast Learning Disability Social Work Team between 1 January 1996 and 31 December 2005 were studied. The documentary analysis of all 252 referrals during the ten-year period included referral books, social work files and the electronic client-based system, Soscare. There were increases in referrals with recorded autism and in those aged 18–25, and high levels of recorded behavioural difficulties. There were low levels of recorded visual impairment, hearing impairment and mental health problems. Twenty-one per cent of referrals were likely to have been diagnosed with a learning disability at age 16 or over. Child referrals showed a broad spectrum of identified need whereas adult referrals were predominantly identified as needing daytime occupation. There was an increase in the team caseload from 364 to 489 over the period caused by the number of referrals exceeding the number of closures every year except 1997. We recommend a greater focus on health status in social work assessments, a review of case management practice and greater inclusion of 'newly diagnosed' adolescents and adults in service planning.

(Morrison et al., 2010)

Mixed methods

Fourthly, if we are faced with the task of 'evaluating a service' we may wish to gather some quantitative data and some qualitative data. For example, we might want numerical data on how many use the service and for how long, and the profile of clients in terms of needs or geographic location. We might also want some verbal (qualitative) data from clients expressing their perception on receiving the service, and from providers on the strengths and limitations of the service from their perspective. This is a simultaneous mixed-methods design. There are also mixed-methods designs that use qualitative data to inform a survey or an experiment, or which use a survey or experiment to inform a qualitative study. These are discussed towards the end of the chapter in the context of knowledge creation processes. Note that a thorough evaluation of a service in terms of its effectiveness in achieving the planned change (in the lives of clients) would need a consideration of the issues discussed in relation to questions of effectiveness. An example of a service evaluation can be seen in the evaluation summary below.

Research summary

Background: Young people with disabilities are often excluded from the labour market. This paper describes a qualitative evaluation of an innovative two-year pilot initiative (VOTE) implemented to provide employment training and support for vulnerable young adults with a wide range of disabilities.

Aims: The principal aims of the study were to assess the impact of the new service in the extent to which: (1) it had created and developed training and employment opportunities for young people; and (2) promoted inclusive working partnerships.

Method: Documentary analysis was used as a basis for describing and assessing the project objectives in combination with face-to-face interviews with a small number of key stakeholders.

Results: A total of 122 young people participated in the initiative in the pilot period during which time 160 qualifications were obtained. Key stakeholders expressed positive views about the initiative and, in particular, its therapeutic benefits and the extent of inter-agency working and shared learning.

Conclusion: The VOTE initiative achieved considerable success in empowering a significant proportion of young adults to engage in society by developing social and employment skills, and by improving their employment opportunities and prospects. Factors critical to the continued success of this and similar initiatives include: the matching of employment and training opportunities to client needs, abilities and aspirations; addressing the concerns of local employers; and the sympathetic treatment of workplace issues.

(Taylor et al., 2004).

Other questions and research designs

There are also important questions about the causes of social problems (social epidemiology) which tend to require longitudinal research designs, about costs and cost-effectiveness of interventions, and about assessment instruments (including prediction, prognosis, validity, reliability and usability) which are beyond the scope of this book. The interested reader is referred to Engel and Schutt (2013), Taylor (2012a) or Thyer (2010) in the Further Reading section.

Activity

This chapter began by stating that the choice of design relates to the question rather than to the topic. To illustrate this, consider the questions below in terms of: What type of question is it? What design is most appropriate? What would need to be clarified to create an answerable question?

- What are the perceptions of older people on hospital discharge arrangements?
- What is the effect on likelihood of returning home of different hospital discharge arrangements?
- What proportion of young people in state care with mental health problems has been sexually abused?
- What is effective in helping sexually abused children to avoid mental health problems in later life?
- How do older people conceptualise elder abuse?
- What is effective in reducing recurrence of elder abuse?
- What is the most effective way to prevent repeated episodes of self-harm amongst adolescents?
- How do adolescents who harm themselves perceive their behaviour?
- Why do (= what are the causative factors that correlate with...) some adolescents repeatedly harm themselves?

These four basic designs are discussed in more detail in appropriate chapters later in this book, as a framework for relating subsequent chapters to appropriate study questions in your environment.

Summary

- Some types of experimental or quasi-experimental design will be most appropriate if we have a question about the effect of a planned intervention. These designs are discussed further in Chapter 6.
- Some types of qualitative design will be most appropriate if we have a question about the perspectives of people, for example, on their needs or their experience of receiving or providing services. Qualitative approaches are discussed further in Chapter 6.
- Some types of survey design will be most appropriate if we wish to know about the prevalence or incidence of some behaviour, attitude or event, including for professional audit purposes. Surveys are discussed further in Chapter 6.

- A simultaneous mixed-method design may be appropriate to give a rounded picture to evaluate a service.
- Inductive research (typically qualitative) and deductive research (typically experiments or surveys) are complementary parts of the process of creating knowledge.
- To create knowledge that will enable us to develop effective social work interventions requires a range of types of research, each suited to its particular purpose.
- Clarify your question before selecting your method:
  - if you want to prove, measure, compare or contrast something you need a quantitative method;
  - if you want to explore experiences, perceptions and conceptualisations to create a new theory or understanding, select a qualitative method.

Further reading

Creswell, JW and Plano Clark, VL (2011) *Designing and Conducting Mixed Methods Research*. London: Sage.

An informative, thorough book on robust approaches to mixed-methods studies.

Engel, RJ and Schutt, RK (2013) *The Practice of Research in Social Work (3rd edition)*. Thousand Oaks, CA: Sage.

This comprehensive text provides detailed material on a range of research designs, including particularly experimental designs.

Fischer, J and Corcoran, K (2007) *Measures for Clinical Practice and Research: A Sourcebook: Vol. 1: Couples, Families, and Children*. New York: Oxford University Press.

Fischer, J and Corcoran, K (2007) *Measures for Clinical Practice and Research: A Sourcebook: Vol. 2: Adults*. New York: Oxford University Press.

These two volumes provide an excellent compendium of assessment tools that social workers can use in their practice with individuals. The term 'clinical' in North America and Australasia is used to denote social workers helping individuals (and groups) to tackle their psychosocial problems in life, rather than community development, safeguarding or care planning.

Taylor, BJ (2012a) 'Intervention Research' (Chapter 27; pp424–439) in Gray, M, Midgley, J and Webb, S (eds) *Social Work Handbook*. New York: Sage.

This chapter outlines the main designs for studying the effectiveness of planned interventions using social work examples, and provides an overview of the main issues including intervention fidelity, defining outcome measures, and the ethical and practical issues in masked random assignment.

Thyer, B (ed) (2010) *The Handbook of Social Work Research Methods (2nd edition)*. Thousand Oaks, CA: Sage.

A valuable book providing a range of perspectives on research methods in social work.

3: Sampling Techniques in Quantitative and Qualitative Research

Chapter aims

This chapter will:

- consider a range of sampling techniques and their relevance to a selection of research designs;
- examine the differences between probability and non-probability sampling techniques;
- discuss a range of probability sampling methods including simple, systematic, stratified, random and cluster sampling;
- consider non-probability designs, for example purposive, quota and snowball sampling techniques.

Introduction

Sampling is a core component of any research project but, unfortunately, it is one that is often misunderstood or misinterpreted by social work undergraduate and postgraduate students as they grapple with the new language and foreign concepts associated with the research process.

However, as a social work research student you must have an understanding of the various types and uses of sampling techniques in order to ensure that your research project is viable and fit for the purpose for which it was designed. There are a number of questions which must be considered before choosing a suitable sampling technique including:

- What is the difference between probability and non-probability sampling?

- Which do I use and why?

- How big does the sample need to be?

- Is it important to have a representative sample?

- Which one of the many sampling techniques is most suited my intended research design?

In some research projects, researchers opt for a *census* approach whereby *all* members of the population are used in the study. The population is the entire group of people or units that the researcher wishes to study. For example, you may wish to seek the views of all first year social work degree students (n = 300) in the two universities in Northern Ireland. It is possible to use a *census method* in this instance as a survey could quite easily be delivered to all of the 300 social work student population in that region.

However, if you wished to study the population of all social work undergraduate students in England, it would be a very onerous task to send out surveys to the entire population of registered students in over 70 institutions which deliver undergraduate social work programmes in the country. Therefore, it would be much easier to obtain a *sample* to gather data from a selected group, which would be chosen in a way that represents the *population* (i.e. all undergraduate social work students from universities in England).

The advantages of using a sample in research include the following:

- in most cases, coverage of the whole population is not possible;

- information is less expensive to collate due to the smaller numbers involved;

- fewer people are needed to gather and interpret the data;

- studies that use samples are quicker to administer;

- in some cases, fewer numbers means it is easier to collect more data and gather more detailed information.

(Burton, 2000; Sarantakos, 2005)

Points to note

A number of undergraduate and postgraduate social work research projects utilise a census approach as they usually wish to study small populations in a specific geographical area. For example, a social worker on a postgraduate research programme explored the views of a small number of carers (n = 20) of children with complex learning disabilities in a Health and Social Care Trust in Northern Ireland. Another undergraduate social work project considered the perceptions of qualified and unqualified social workers in six residential care homes in a specified location (n = 36). In both projects, it was not necessary to construct a sample due to the small numbers of respondents available to the respective research students.

Distinctions between probability and non-probability sampling

Fundamentally, there are two primary types of sampling; probability sampling and non-probability sampling. The former, also known as random sampling, is primarily used within quantitative research and has a number of strict rules associated with its use which permit inferences to be made to the wider population it represents (i.e. the findings from research which uses probability sampling can make claims about the wider population it represents).

Probability sampling claims representativeness of the population from which it is drawn and usually, but not always, relies on large numbers either in surveys or experimental designs such as random controlled trials. The underpinning premise of probability sampling is that the researcher considers data from the sample with the goal of making inferences about the whole population from which the sample is drawn. A core principle is that everyone within the target population has an equal chance of being chosen for the sample. In order to do this, it is important to have a complete list of the population, which is known as the sampling *frame*, from which the sample is selected using a specific technique. This is usually achieved with the help of a computer-generated programme or a random number table.

De Vaus (1996) highlights the differences between both probability and non-probability sampling procedures in a succinct manner:

> *A probability sample is one in which each person in the population has an equal, or at least a known chance (probability) of being selected while in a non-probability sample some people have a greater, but unknown, chance than others of selection.*

(De Vaus 1996, p60)

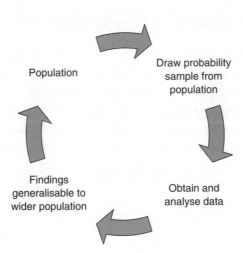

Figure 3.1   The probability sample cycle in social research

More generally, the sampling plan must be clearly delineated with the research aims and objectives and, thus, if the research demands representativeness, then a probability sampling technique must be employed. However, if you wish to study the views and perceptions of the respondents in more detail as part of the original aims and objectives, then a non-probability sampling technique is more likely to precipitate results that will engender the best research outcomes. Non-probability samples are most usually associated with qualitative research; they do not claim representativeness of the wider population and, generally speaking, have smaller numbers and are usually used for exploratory or in-depth analysis of a specific social issue or topic.

Activity

A postgraduate social work student intends to study the levels of resilience in child protection social workers who have just finished a programme of assessed and supported year in employment (ASYE, a probationary period introduced for newly qualified social workers in Northern Ireland in a target population n = 270). Concomitantly, she wishes to look at the levels of resilience in child protection social workers who have been in practice for three to five years (target population = 380). She is using specific measuring tools for resilience with both subgroups of social workers.

- Should the student use a total census method or a sample technique to obtain her respondents?
- If a sample is required, should this be a probability or non-probability sample?
- Give reasons for your answers.

Probability sampling in quantitative research

Social researchers employ probability sampling for a range of reasons, including its reliability, generalisability, representativeness and facilitation of the use of inferential statistics. Researchers use inferential statistics to make sense of quantitative data and to consider relationships between a number of different variables. For example, you might wish to look at the relationship between gender and bullying in young people within residential care and statistical tests will help you determine the possible occurrence and strength of that relationship.

A number of principles may be applied to the application of probability sampling:

- the population must be clearly defined;
- the selection process should be governed by clear exclusion and inclusion criteria;

- sample units must be easily identifiable and clearly defined;
- sample units must be independent of each other and the same units should be used, throughout the study;
- incorrect sampling will seriously undermine research findings.

(Henry, 1990; Burton, 2000; Sarantakos, 2005)

Example – Probability sampling

Researchers wished to find out about the alcohol use of students aged 13–18 years in schools within a defined geographical area. Rather than ask *all* the young people in *all* schools within the designated area (population roughly 42,000), researchers obtained a probability sample using a specific mathematical technique. In doing so, all young people had an equal chance of being chosen for the survey. Therefore, the researchers could claim that the results from the survey were representative of the views of the 42,000 in the target population.

Table 3.1 indicates a typology of probability sampling techniques which are discussed in the following section, with examples used to illustrate their use in the research process.

Simple random sampling

In this procedure all cases (usually people) within the chosen population have an equal chance of being selected via a range of methods, a few of which are described below.

The lottery method of simple random sampling

A simple random sample is an unbiased representation of a group of people (such as a specific group of social work service users) or units (a number of social work case files). The lottery

Table 3.1 A typology of probability sampling techniques

Sampling technique	Selection strategy
Simple random	Each member of the target population – computer programme or mathematical list of numbers are used.
Systematic	A population is compiled, members are chosen at equal intervals and a random start is designated.
Stratified	Each member of the population is assigned to a sub-group and then a simple random selection technique is employed to select people from each group.
Cluster	Each population member is assigned to a group or cluster, clusters are selected at random and all members of selected clusters are included in the sample.

Source: Henry, 1990, p27

method uses a sample design, whereby names are simply replaced by numbers and chosen at random from a container.

Example – Lottery method of random sampling

A researcher wishes to obtain a simple random sample of 30 older people social workers from a population of 300 employed by a County Council. The list comprising the names of all 300 workers represents the sampling frame. The list may then be converted into numbers (represented on pieces of paper) and these are placed in a container. The numbers are then drawn at random and the corresponding name in the sampling frame is obtained. This continues until the required number is reached.

Most cases of simple random sampling occur *without replacement,* i.e. once the number has been drawn it is not returned to the hat. It is also acceptable to return the number to the hat, known as a *selection with replacement* strategy, although this may give the unfavourable effect of the reselection of a number of cases (Burton, 2000).

Computer-generated method of simple random sampling

This is similar to the method described above but replaces the container with a computer-generated database of numbers. For example, the computer is programmed to generate a set of numbers between one and 1,000 and then randomly selects the required sample. This is often the preferred method of sampling in research which uses large numbers and is less time consuming than the lottery method.

Systematic sampling

Systematic sampling is used when the researcher knows how many people or cases are within the sampling frame and has defined the sample size required. As the name suggests, the sampling process is conducted in a systematic fashion often using a sampling fraction to determine the choice of sample. For example, if the target population is 600 and the researcher wishes to obtain a sample of 200, the simple sampling fraction is $600/200 = 3$. This indicates that every third person would be chosen from the sampling frame. The starting point for the first selection is chosen at random.

Example – Systemic sampling

Within a multi-stage audit of decision making in child protection social work, one phase of the research programme focused on an analysis of phone calls made to an initial assessment team over a five-month period. The analysis considered what decisions were made as a result

$\longrightarrow$

---

of the initial referral call. The sampling frame was comprised of 820 phone calls made to the unit within the specified time period and the researchers wished to sample 400 of the calls made (820/400=2.05). Therefore, the researchers considered every other phone call choosing a number at random to begin the process.

However, some caution must be employed when using this method as the list may reflect a trend in how the data is stored. For example, if it was a list of family members according to age, with oldest to youngest, and a fifth fraction was calculated, the sample maybe overrepresented by younger members of the family unit.

Stratified random sampling

This is a modified form of simple or systematic sampling with an additional layer built into the process. Initially, there is stratification (or layering) of the sample according to certain groups – age, gender or ethnic identity, etc. – with a sample subsequently drawn from each of the groups chosen. In addition, the sample size may be proportionate or disproportionate to the target population, i.e. a greater percentage may be drawn from one of the groups according to the objectives of the research and the special interests of the researcher. The individual samples are then amalgamated and this makes up the sample for the research project.

Example – Stratified random sampling

A social work research programme considered the perceptions of migrant workers in Northern Ireland as regards alcohol and substance abuse problems experienced by migrant populations. Three ethnic groups were chosen: Lithuanian, Polish and Portuguese. It was decided that a dispro-portionate sample from the groups would be drawn with the ratio: Polish 60 per cent, Lithuanian 20 per cent and Portuguese 20 per cent. This disproportionate figure was decided upon as the Polish community represents the greatest majority of immigrant workers in the region.

Cluster sampling

Cluster sampling is used when it is very difficult to identify a specific sampling frame, usually as a result of the large numbers in the population and also when economic constraints are evident. For example, it would be difficult to construct a sampling frame of social workers in older people teams throughout England and Wales, Scotland and Northern Ireland, in a study which intended to collate their views of provision of services for older people with dementia.

It must be noted that cluster sampling is biased, as respondents are obtained from pre-selected groups such as schools/classes as in the example described below. Therefore, they will not represent the full extent of the target population.

Example - Cluster sampling

A social work research student intends to study the effect of family structure on the drug use of young people in Northern Ireland. A list of all grammar, private and state secondary schools is obtained from the Department of Education in Northern Ireland. Schools are chosen from the sampling frame by means of a computer-generated random sample process. The number of pupils for inclusion in the study is determined and then divided by the number of schools to ascertain the number of pupils to be chosen from each school. The sampling frame is determined from each school and the required number of respondents chosen using a random computer-generated method. The number of all students chosen in this manner makes up the sample.

An overview of errors in social research

There are two main categories of errors in social research; *non-sampling errors* and *sampling errors*.

Non-sampling errors may be due to response errors, when respondents provide wrong information, perhaps due to the provision of clearly dishonest answers or a lack of understanding of the questions. Non-sampling errors may also be as a result of interviewer errors as a result of leading questioning style and/or mistakes in the recording of the information. Problems may also arise as a result of researcher error during coding or data entry. The most common non-sampling error, however, is that related to non-response errors.

Non-response errors

Non-response error is most commonly witnessed in survey research and there are various reasons as to why this happens, including respondents' unwillingness to complete the survey, respondents' unavailability at the time of administration of the survey, or the inability to respond to the survey for other reasons, such as poor literacy. Low non-response rates (of 25 per cent or below) present problems in that the final sample may be not be representative of the original intended sample. However, it is difficult to determine in what ways the non-responses are biased and therefore it is difficult to address this specific issue (Gerrish and Lacey, 2006).

One method of counteracting the loss of respondents is to conduct a pilot study to gauge the estimated drop out and the level of understanding of the questions within the survey. Some researchers choose to ignore the loss of respondents, particularly if the response rate is high, although this is controversial with many researchers arguing that substitution is necessary once all possible methods of recruiting the non-respondents have been exhausted (Sarantakos, 2005). In the social work research field, this problem may be ameliorated to some extent via the careful and systematic planning of the research process and having some prior knowledge of the intended population.

Examples – Addressing non-response errors

1. A former child protection social worker undertaking a PhD research programme was aware that it would be difficult to persuade busy frontline social workers to complete a quite detailed survey and accompanying psychometric tools to measure stress. In order to counteract the expected high non-return rate, she travelled around the selected offices and presented the questionnaire to members of the chosen sample at the least busy time of the working day.

2. A postgraduate research student used postal and follow-up online surveys to request the return of a questionnaire from student social workers on placement. This was accompanied by regular updates as regards the numbers of student colleagues from other social work offices who had returned questionnaires in larger numbers. The employment of a tenacious approach which harnessed a sense of competitiveness within the student population produced a respectable response rate.

Sampling errors

Sampling errors are inherent to the sample selection process and may either be represented through systematic or random errors. The former, systematic errors, may occur when the selection process was not entirely random, (i.e. there was a mistake in the randomisation process) or the sample was not drawn from a list of the whole population. Random errors may be present due to sample size; when the sample size is large there are fewer random errors as it is more likely to represent the population from which it was taken.

Non-probability sampling

Non-probability sampling is used for a variety of reasons in both quantitative and qualitative research. In quantitative studies it may be used where time or money are limited or as part of a pilot study or an exploratory study. It may also be used where there are difficulties associated with compiling a sampling frame from a 'hidden' population, such as homeless drug users. The disadvantages of using non-probability methods within quantitative studies are based on the premise that they do not claim representativeness and we cannot generalise the results of the study to the wider population as the sample has not been chosen in a random fashion.

In qualitative design studies, the non-probability method is accepted as this method does not claim representativeness and, therefore, does not require a complex sampling frame or calculation to determine sample size.

There is a range of non-probability sampling techniques including quota, purposive, snowball and respondent-driven sampling. Table 3.2 indicates the use of the sampling methods according to research methodology.

Table 3.2 Non-probability research design sampling techniques

Sampling technique	Quantitative	Qualitative
Quota	Yes	Not usual
Purposive	Yes	Yes
Snowball	Yes	Yes
Event/spatial	Yes	No
Respondent	Yes	No

Quota sampling

Quota sampling is a non-random stratified sampling procedure often used as a market research technique and uses 'quotas' as set by the researcher. The researcher sets the criteria as regards inclusion in the research, for example, age, gender or ethnicity. A researcher may send a number of interviewers into a shopping centre to interview a specific number of mums with infants in prams or older people who are using walking aids. Another student researcher may stand outside a university crèche over the course of the day and interview only male students to obtain their views on childcare facilities within the university. Quota sampling is cost effective and less restrictive in terms of time required for planning and administration. However, it is obviously highly susceptible to problems of researcher bias, is not representative and findings are not generalisable.

Activity

Consider the following:

- Would this be a useful technique to employ for a small-scale student research project?
- Using your own research idea as an example, note the pros and cons of using this type of sampling method.
- What levels of bias could be introduced when using this method?

Purposive sampling

This technique is often used when researchers wish to target specific sections of society as they are deemed to be relevant to the research topic. It is used in political polling or by various forms of media to elicit the views of certain sections of the population. It is apparent that this form of sample technique used within the world of media or political polling may 'harness' a particular viewpoint according to the people chosen, the current political or social climate and/or the questions used.

Purposive sampling is often used in small-scale qualitative research studies to obtain the perceptions of a specific group of people relevant to the aims and objectives of the research. Many research students using qualitative methods find this to be the most straightforward method of obtaining their sample and find it easy to choose their participants based on the nature and purpose of their research project.

Example – Purposive sampling

A postgraduate research student wished to gather the views of professionals (social workers, counsellors and other related professionals who provided bereavement care) as regards their experience of providing bereavement care for families following the death of a family member. The researcher chose 15 health care professionals in one Health and Social Care Trust in Northern Ireland who had provided bereavement counselling or care after the death of a close family relative. The professionals were chosen specifically as a result of their work experience in the area of bereavement care and subsequently to gather their views on the definitions of bereavement care, the different types of bereavement models used and improvements that could be made in multi-disciplinary working.

Snowball sampling

It is often difficult for both experienced and non-experienced researchers to obtain a sample of research respondents from what is known as a 'hidden population'. It is difficult to construct a sampling frame when the parameters of the population are unknown to the researcher.

It may be difficult to access a group of people as a result of their experiences of discrimination or injustice (e.g. asylum seekers, homeless people or specific ethnic minorities). In addition, other groups may be inherently mistrusting of the researcher (e.g, offenders or drug users) because of the implications of providing information to a third party regarding criminal activity.

In snowball sampling the researcher may begin by interviewing one or two key informants who are immediately available to them. During interviews they ask the participants to identify others who could be included in the research as a result of the commonality of the research focus, such as drug misuse. This invitation process is continued until a saturation point has been reached, at a number determined by the researcher.

Example – Snowball sampling

A postgraduate research student wished to conduct a qualitative study of the views of Irish Traveller men in relation to their physical and mental health. A number of key male travellers known to the researcher were approached and asked to identify male travellers who were living in non-settled travelling sites and who were part of the transient population (a population which was impossible to quantify). The men who agreed to take part in the project were then asked to recommend other possible respondents. This process was continued until the researcher engaged with fifteen respondents, a number deemed acceptable for the objectives of the small-scale project.

Research summary

Respondent-driven sampling (moving from a non-probability to a probability snowball sampling technique)

Respondent-driven sampling (RDS) is a relatively new sampling method which builds upon snowball sampling and has been used widely in a number of studies with hidden populations such as drug users (Abdul-Quader et al., 2006) and HIV respondents (Malekinejad et al., 2008). RDS uses the same 'seed' technique as snowball sampling but frames the process within a mathematical model that weights the sample to counteract the non-random nature of the sampling technique. The RDS model utilises the advantages of the snowball sampling technique whilst facilitating the generalisability of the results from the data to the wider estimated population (see Wejnert and Heckathorn, 2011 for further discussion of the technique).

Theoretical sampling

Theoretical sampling (Glaser and Strauss, 1967; Bryman, 2004; Flick, 2006) is used in qualitative research designs in which the researcher chooses people or units to develop and test theoretical constructs. The researcher chooses a sample, gathers and analyses the data and subsequently chooses a sample to further consider the emerging categories and theories. This technique is continued until the researcher reaches theoretical saturation point, i.e. no further new categories or sub-categories of information are emergent from the data. Flick (2006) also highlights that it is crucial to define the criteria for choosing the incremental sample with the theory from the data being used effectively to identify the subsequent participants in the research process. Strauss and Corbin (1998) highlight the use of unstructured sampling techniques at the beginning of the process with more structured approaches such as purposive sampling being utilised at later stages in the data gathering process to enhance the opportunities for comparisons to be made.

This particular technique is seldom used in undergraduate and post-qualifying research studies but is usually employed at PhD and post-doctoral levels.

What is a good sample size?

This question, more than any other, preoccupies the mind of student researchers when they are designing their research project. Invariably, there is the view that bigger is better, whether the research project is qualitative or quantitative. However, it must be acknowledged that the concept of representativeness is key to the choice of sample size. As stated earlier, qualitative purposive samples do not claim representativeness and, therefore, do not require large numbers or statistical calculations to determine size. The size of the sample is calculated by the researcher to suit the purpose of the research design.

Quantitative surveys, which involve non-probability snowball or quota sampling, do not produce generalisable findings and, again, do not require statistical calculation methods to work out the required size. The magic number to allow for statistical inferences to be made appears to be (n=100), a figure which seems to be quoted often by social work research students. However, many researchers purport that this is not correct and some statistical measures are designed for samples which are less than 30 (Sarantakos, 2005). That said, the use of a representative sample, using a random sampling design, must determine the size of the sample to claim representativeness from the population from which it was drawn.

Whilst there are no definitive answers to this question, there are a few guidelines offered by a range of researcher authors.

- Qualitative research usually uses smaller sample sizes. The nature of the enquiry is localised, focused and engenders a depth of data – NOT representativeness.

- As a social work student researcher, consider the time constraints and the collection, analysis and write up of data; more gathered information does not always mean a higher-quality project.

- Exploratory quantitative studies may use smaller samples (i.e. ≥ 30,) if the population is homogenous with the respect to the study object.

- However, it is generally recognised that the larger the sample size in quantitative research, the greater the degree of accuracy and representativeness. The sampling error is reduced according with the increase in the sample size.

- Conversely, larger samples do not always *singularly* provide a high degree of validity or precision. It must be noted that sample size is only one of many factors that will lead to a successful study.

(Burton, 2000; De Vaus, 1996; Howitt and Cramer, 2008; Sarantakos, 2005)

Summary

This chapter has focused on:

- the methods of sampling most often used by social work student researchers at undergraduate and postgraduate levels;
- the difference between probability and non-probability sampling and their uses within quantitative and qualitative research projects;
- the categories of probability sampling, how they are employed in practice and the most appropriate context in which to use this type of sampling technique;
- sampling errors in social research, subdividing the categories in to non-sampling and sampling errors;
- the use of a number of probability sampling methods, and the ways in which they could be utilised both in quantitative and qualitative research studies;
- the integral debate as regards the 'size' of the sample and the presentation of some helpful suggestions from other sources for discussion;
- case examples from 'real' social work students' research, demonstrating the use of the range of probability and non-probability techniques in practice.

Further reading

Rubin, A and Babbie, C (2010) *Essential Research Methods in Social Work*. Belmont CA: Brooks/Cole, Cengage Learning.

Flick, U (2006) *An Introduction to Qualitative Research*. Thousand Oaks, CA: Sage.

Williams, M and Paul Vogt, W (2011) *The Sage Handbook of Innovation in Social Research Methods*. London: Sage.

4: Qualitative Data Gathering

Chapter aims

This chapter will:

- focus on the planning and data gathering stages of qualitative research, and the qualitative aspect of audit and service evaluation projects;
- consider the essential features of qualitative methods and the context in which they are appropriate;
- explore ways of preparing and conducting interviews and focus groups, including:
  - practical preparation issues such as location and timing;
  - tuning in to the participant(s) – whether clients or staff – and their context; and
  - preparing an aide-memoire for interviewing and for conducting focus groups.
- offer some notes on observation, diaries and documentary analysis, data gathering methods which are used less commonly in social work research.

Introduction and definitions

In this chapter, the processes of facilitating semi-structured interviews and focus groups are discussed in the context of adapting basic social work therapeutic communication skills. Consideration of particular qualitative designs (such as grounded theory, interpretative phenomenological analysis, etc.) is beyond the scope of this book which is targeted at undergraduate and master's degree dissertation level, where basic thematic analysis is generally regarded as sufficiently complex (cf. Starks and Trinidad, 2007; Taylor et al.,

2015). Engaging others to conduct the interviews or focus groups, and engaging service users as co-researchers (e.g. to co-conduct interviews or focus groups) are regarded as beyond the scope of projects at this level, although we encourage engaging service users in other ways. Qualitative methods may also be used within professional audit and service evaluation projects. The analysis of qualitative data is the focus of Chapter 7; this chapter focuses on the earlier stages of the process.

The purpose of qualitative research is to create an understanding of the meanings and perceptions of some group or 'type' of people in relation to a relatively unexplored topic. In terms of generalisable research, this is in order to create a theory or conceptual way of understanding this aspect of 'their world'. In social work this is likely to be the 'world' of those in need and of those receiving or providing social care (including social work) services including the 'social world' in which the service is received. Respondents may be foster parents, home care workers and those working in residential and day care facilities as well as social workers and clients (including children) receiving these types of services. Qualitative research may be justified because there is limited previous research on the topic and because we wish to understand the context of their 'real-world' in so far as it is relevant for developing services. The focus of qualitative research is on concepts, meanings, perspectives and social processes such as daily living, working life and service provision. These aspects are explored through the language that people speak (or write in some other types of qualitative research) although it is not the language itself that is our interest. Qualitative research may be used to 'test out' a theory, but is not used for theory testing in a pure sense as in deductive quantitative research. As discussed in Chapter 3, qualitative research is essentially inductive research when viewed from within a broader framework of knowledge creation. The place of qualitative research is to help us to build a theory, a model or an understanding of some social process or experience, typically in this case the need-journey, or the receipt or provision of social care services.

Qualitative methods are increasingly used in service evaluation and professional audit to add flesh and blood to what might otherwise be seem to some to be rather lifeless (quantitative) survey data. Illustrating quantitative data in this way is becoming increasingly common in government-sponsored evaluations in various spheres of public activity. Material in this chapter will also be relevant to this more limited use of qualitative methods. Qualitative research typically uses interviews, focus groups, direct observation, documentary analysis and diaries for data gathering; we explain these in turn.

We are using the term 'interview' to mean a planned interactive process between a researcher and a respondent for the purpose of gathering data about perceptions, meanings and understandings of the respondent's experience. This is distinct from a social work interview designed as a helping or therapeutic process. The interview will have some structure which will relate to the research question and previous research on the topic. However, it will not be a series of totally structured questions with closed nominal or scaled responses, such as in an interviewer-administered quantitative survey (see Chapter 6). A blank box following a prompt within a survey – such as in many service evaluations and professional audits – may be regarded as gathering qualitative data. However, it will be apparent that the lack of interaction to prompt and explore perceptions and experiences will limit the richness of data compared to qualitative research per se. The discussion in the interview is structured to obtain perceptions, understandings and meanings on a defined topic in a supportive and open environment. The use of interviews for qualitative research is discussed in detail below.

A focus group in qualitative research is essentially the group work equivalent of an individual interview. A focus group for research purposes is distinct from social group work designed as a helping or therapeutic process. Focus groups usually involve six to 12 people in each session. Typically, participants are involved in a single session lasting perhaps an hour or an hour and a half as well as some time for refreshments and some socialising. However, for more intense or developmental topics participants may take part in more than one session. As with an interview, the discussion in the focus group session is structured to obtain perceptions, understandings and meanings on a defined topic in a supportive and open environment. The use of focus group for qualitative research is discussed in detail below.

Direct observation is used in ethnographic studies, where non-intrusiveness is emphasised so that people can be observed in their normal life (including work) contexts. The emphasis in direct observation is to get close to reality (to achieve external validity) (Floersch et al., 2014). Social work examples might be studying the experience of substance abuse amongst people with mental illness or the experience of poverty amongst single parents.

Documentary analysis is where documents (diaries, letters, biographies, organisational communications, government reports, websites, blogs, etc.) are viewed as both constructing and describing lived realities. Of interest is how the communication came into being, its purpose and readership, underpinning ideas, theories and assumptions, and the social and organisational context in which it was written.

Activity

Trace, through documents, the evolution of the language (and hence concepts) used in respect of:

- battered baby syndrome (1950s);
- non-accidental injury (1960s–70s);
- child abuse (1980s);
- child abuse and neglect (1990s);
- safeguarding children (2000s);
- child exploitation (2010s).

Documentary analysis should not be confused with literature reviewing as discussed in Chapter 1.

Diaries may also be used as a complement to interviewing, so as to gather extensive contemporaneous data for discussion during the interview. This is valuable where detail of daily living is of interest. A social work example is a study of loneliness amongst older people, where respondents were asked to keep a diary of relevant issues which were discussed in interviews approximately two weeks apart.

Why and when to use qualitative research

The essential issues in selecting a research method to suit the research question are discussed in Chapter 2. Qualitative studies are essentially inductive research. In this context as an aspect of knowledge creation, qualitative studies have an essential place in stimulating new concepts and generating research hypotheses. Interviews and focus groups may be used as data collection tools to elicit views and opinions on services and to assist in the design of tools such as assessment and audit tools. Qualitative research may have a crucial place in the shaping of constructs and use of language in preparation for the design of questionnaires or other data extraction tools for quantitative research. Similarly, qualitative research may be used within mixed methods to explore anomalies and interesting results from surveys and experiments.

Qualitative research is suitable when we want to understand better the lived experience of our respondents, and how this has shaped their perceptions of life or work, or service provision or service receipt. For this reason the focus of the questions in the interview or focus group should relate to the actual experience of participants. Qualitative research is not suited for addressing questions of prevalence, correlation or measurement of difference (for which see Chapter 6). Nor are qualitative methods suited for ascertaining the effectiveness of an intervention, although qualitative methods might be used to explore people's perceptions of the effects of an intervention or the process of receiving it, or to explore their experience of the process of taking part in an experimental study of the effectiveness of an intervention.

The experience of conducting qualitative research is that it is not as linear as quantitative research. There is a greater interplay between data gathering and analysis than in deductive research, as the process of exploration of new concepts, ideas and relationships takes place. The focus is on gathering data in natural settings, including the workplace and situations where people receive services. The aim is to capture data from the insider's perspective, so issues of creating openness and honesty about matters that are generally less public assumes importance.

Interviews and focus groups enable the exploration of data about feelings and beliefs, attitudes and fears, hopes and opinions. Human beings are vast storehouses of information and the researcher wishes to tap into this. Qualitative research does not necessarily require large numbers as the essential issue in sampling is that respondents are 'information rich', i.e. they know and understand the topic from their lived experience, and are able to articulate this to the researcher. The main focus of interviews and focus groups is to explore concepts as expressed in words. However, on some occasions it is also useful to identify non-verbal aspects of responses.

A weakness of interviews and focus groups is that people can lie, or say things to portray themselves in a good light. They may be afraid of offending the interviewer or others in the focus group. For example, people might agree on high-minded principles that they think will please the interviewer, but in reality act differently. Care must be exercised in drawing inferences about qualitative data. For example, people criticising services as part of a study does not mean that they will voice or lodge a complaint with the service provider. The researcher needs to explicitly reflect on possible biases such as these as part of the reflective process required within qualitative research. This will be discussed further in Chapter 7.

As well as providing rich data from respondents in their own words, the interaction process in a focus group allows clarification of issues and probing through the dynamic in the group. This can be a stimulating process, going beyond the initial knowledge base and expectations of the conductor of the group. It is important, therefore, to attend to the group interaction in the way that the group is conducted, so as to generate and build on responses from participants.

An important consideration with interviews and focus groups is that they will involve small numbers, and the findings will not be generalisable to a wider population in the way that a survey or experiment might be. The essential point, however, is that qualitative research is essentially inductive, that is to say it is about building a general understanding or theoretical model of the typical meaning, experience or world view of respondents. Qualitative methods are not suited to measuring the prevalence of some characteristic among a population; for that a survey would be required. The strength of qualitative research is to create the concepts, language and anchor points for scales that might be used within a survey as discussed in Chapter 6.

The conduct of an interview or focus group plays a key role in the validity of the data gathering. If an open, trusting relationship is not created then the responses will lose the very aspect that gives qualitative research its strength: accessing the world as perceived by respondents. If an individual is allowed to dominate a focus group session then the data will not be so true of the perceptions of other respondents both because they have had less time to speak and perhaps because they might be less likely to speak what they truly feel. The liveliness of the debate does not necessarily mean that the data has good credibility, although often it is the case that the most pertinent issues for exploration ignite engaged discussion and create rich data. A poorly facilitated interview or focus group can lead respondents to provide what they perceive as the 'desired comment' rather than speaking honestly. Attention by the interviewer or focus group leader to these aspects is crucial for high quality qualitative research, as explored further below.

Preparing for interviews and focus groups

One asset of focus groups is that one can obtain rich data from a larger number of respondents relatively quickly compared to separate interviews. However, for the purposes of considering sampling numbers, one cannot simply add up the total number of respondents across groups and regard that as the sample size. Due to the interplay between respondents, researchers cannot treat the total number as if they were individual interviewees just because they happened to gather the data from them in a more efficient group manner. Some researchers consider that it is the number of focus group sessions that must be considered as the sample size. A general rule of thumb is that a focus group session should consist of between six and twelve people to increase the likelihood of everyone contributing.

The purpose of the interview or focus group needs to be explained clearly as part of the recruitment process, and normally the ethics committee will require this to be in written form. This participant information will need to explain the affiliation of the researcher and any funding body for the research or educational programme of which it is a part. The statement of purpose in the participant information sheet will then form the basis for the statement of purpose used for the opening of the interview or focus group.

Careful consideration needs to be given to the timing of sessions in social work research. Social workers and other social care staff will not respond as readily or as fully when they are under time pressures at work, such as on Friday afternoons or in the run-up to the Christmas holidays. In regard to older people it may be important to think carefully – and discuss with appropriate professionals or facility managers – about the most appropriate time of day to conduct a session. Building a focus group session around the morning coffee break in a residential or supported living facility can often work well.

Example – Practical aspects of preparing for a focus group

Data was sought in relation to sheltered housing provision for older people through ten focus groups with tenants. Each of the 19 sheltered housing schemes in the area was sent a letter inviting them to take part, together with an information sheet explaining the background of the study, its aims and objectives. Following the letter, the managers of the sheltered housing schemes were contacted by telephone and invited to take part. The aim was to convene a focus group of tenants for one scheme operated by each organisation where they operated on more than one site. Housing scheme managers were asked to give an information sheet to each tenant prior to the visit by the researcher inviting them to take part in a focus group session. The focus group sessions were normally arranged to coincide

→

with the weekly coffee morning to suit the tenants' routine. The researcher explained to tenants the aims of the study and asked if they were happy to proceed. At this point the issues of confidentiality and legitimacy of varied opinions were addressed. All focus groups were recorded and transcribed, with the consent of the participants. Topics included the process of moving in and moving on, management of residents' care needs, gaps in current provision, what might be done to overcome these gaps and aspects of provision that could be improved. Each topic had prompt questions to explore tenants' opinions. Focus group sessions normally lasted about 60 minutes.

(Adapted from Taylor and Neill, 2009)

The location of the interview or focus group session needs careful attention. Issues such as personal safety, privacy, confidentiality and disabled access need to be considered. It may be that the individual's own home is most appropriate for some studies and least appropriate for others. The local culture may convey a message that makes a particular venue very appropriate or not at all appropriate. Unless the study is conducted within a residential or day care facility, then access issues such as public transport and car parking need to be considered. If the research involves clients as participants, then do they need assistance to participate, and what particular needs do they have? If the study involves carers, will they need relief from their caring in order to participate? Some modest funding may be required to make aspirations in this regard a reality.

Within the venue attention needs to be given to access and toilet facilities, and ways to create a relaxed yet work-like environment. The seating arrangement needs to be considered just as in social work interviewing or group work. What seating arrangement will facilitate the sharing of views so that everyone can see everyone else (in a focus group) and will provide opportunity for healthy exchange but not tend to provoke hostile confrontation?

The sequence of events from the participant(s) arriving or you arriving with the participant(s) needs to be carefully thought through. Will you allow some time for socialising at the start to 'break the ice'? For focus group sessions it is valuable to try to help people to relax as they arrive and it is common to provide some refreshments to ease this socialising process if people do not know each other. If the focus group session is being run within a residential or day care facility where people already know each other, and should arrive within a short space of time of each other, it may be more appropriate to provide some light refreshments at the end. For interviews there tends to be more variation in such matters. If you are visiting a client in their own home, or a professional in their office, you may be offered a cup of tea. If you are inviting them to your organisation's premises you may offer a cup of coffee as a small token of thanks as well as to ease the way in to a working research relationship. In general, you might expect an interview to last about one hour, and a focus group session about 90 minutes. If you are supplying refreshments this will probably add additional time to a focus group, whereas a cup of tea can be consumed during an interview.

It is important that the interviewer or leader of the focus group prepares for the participants in terms of 'tuning in' as it is commonly called in terms of social work practice. There is occasionally a misunderstanding that because some schools of qualitative research talk about beginning with a 'blank slate', that preliminary reading of literature and tuning in should not be undertaken. However, people who do not prepare adequately for the topics likely to be discussed and the issues likely to be of concern or interest to participants would not make a good interviewer or focus group leader. If you do not tune in, you are less likely to be alert to more subtle expression of issues and the underpinning emotion. The message about commencing with a *tabula rasa* that is emphasised in some schools of qualitative research refers rather to avoiding dictating the structure of the questioning and of the analysis of data according to a preconceived theoretical perspective. This is common to most qualitative approaches. You are generally seeking to elicit the world view of participants. To do this you need to be tuned in to possible issues and nuances, but without imposing your own conceptualisation. The aide-memoire will generally be structured around open questions to guide the topic for discussion. The prompts for more focused questions will only be used if the respondent does not pick up this aspect in their reply to the open question. Even then, the prompts will be in common language and will generally allow for a variety of understandings rather than using particular theoretical constructs. Tuning in, as in social work practice (Taylor and Devine, 1993), might be in relation to:

- the respondents in general in terms of issues in their families and communities;
- the respondents in relation to the topic for which they are being interviewed or brought together, and how it might impact on their lives; and
- the respondents in relation to arriving at the session and what their feelings might be about how the session will be conducted.

You should also consider any risks to yourself as the researcher (cf. Taylor, 2011); an aspect of the study which may be required to be clarified as part of the research governance approval process.

Preparing an aide-memoire of questions and prompts

You will normally prepare an aide-memoire of about five to ten questions to ensure consistency across the interviews and focus groups that you are conducting. Questions are generally ordered from more general to more specific so as to make most sense to the interviewee or focus group member. You would generally avoid putting the most sensitive or most important questions at the beginning so as to give people time to get used to the interview or focus group process and to trust the interviewer or group.

The literature review should directly inform the aide-memoire for the interview or focus group session as well as the tuning in discussed above. A sound approach is to create a table indicating which particular previous studies informed which parts of the aide-memoire. The previous literature on the topic will also form the basis for tuning in to the interview or focus group participants, just as in social work practice (Shulman, 2009).

Generally the aide-memoire will contain about five to ten 'grand tour' open questions that cover the topics of interest. Prompts are constructed in relation to each topic so that if the respondent does not include comment on some particular aspect in response to the open questions, a more focused follow up prompt question can be used. Although we are not aiming to cover particular qualitative methods in this book, it is worth mentioning that within grounded theory, these prompts may be adapted or augmented as the interviews or focus groups proceed. This enables a richer cumulative effect from the process of data gathering, as comments from previous respondents may be presented (anonymously) to subsequent participants for elaboration or challenge. The interested reader is referred to Strauss and Corbin (1990). Note, however, that the basic structure of open grand tour questions is retained throughout, and the introduction to each topic with each respondent is very open in order to gather their unprompted perspective. If you adopt this cumulative approach you might describe your study as 'drawing on elements of grounded theory method'.

Example – 'Grand tour' questions and prompts

1) *Could you tell me about your work assessing older people for care outside their own home?*

   a) What is your role in assessing older people for institutional or home care?

   b) In what circumstances do you think a person requires institutional care?

   c) Do you weigh or assess the seriousness of possible harms and if so, how?

   d) Are the potential benefits or advantages of a course of action a consideration?

2) *Could you tell me about forming a professional judgement about the need for an older person to have care outside the home?*

   a) What assessment tools do you use to assess risk and make decisions?

   b) What is most and least useful about such assessment tools and systems?

   c) Is there a level of 'risk' that is 'acceptable', and if so what is it?

3) *Could you tell me about communicating about risks and decisions with clients, families and other professionals?*

   a) What is your role in communicating with the patient or client about risk?

   b) How do you communicate with other professionals about concerns?

$\longrightarrow$

4) *Could you tell me about how you might handle these decision scenarios?*

    a) Wanting to stay at home despite professional opinion for institutional care.

    b) Wanting institutional care but not deemed to warrant public funding.

    c) Eligible for home care but where circumstances might be harmful to staff.

    d) Wanting to take rehabilitative actions that professionals regard as 'risky'.

(Adapted from a study by Taylor and Donnelly, 2006a)

Piloting

Just as in quantitative studies, piloting is a valuable preparatory stage in qualitative research. Some words, phrases and sentences mean different things to different people. Piloting can help to make the researcher more aware of this. Those participating in the pilot may highlight ways in which the order of the questions might be improved or how an additional question or prompt might help to clarify the question so that a more focused answer may be given. Piloting should be undertaken with a person or people who are similar in essential characteristics to those from whom you are gathering data. However, none of the actual respondents in the study should have the burden of also taking part in the pilot. For a qualitative study this is often less problematic than with a survey where a census sample might be desired. It may be helpful to go to similar respondents in another organisation or geographical area for the piloting if the potential sample for the study is small and you do not want to lose any of them to the piloting process.

Data recording

It will be apparent that to be able to make best use of what respondents say during the interviews or focus groups, it will be necessary to record these effectively. A recording system that records speech clearly is essential. Handwritten notes may help focus your mind on key issues and ensure that you remember to follow up some point later in the session. However, for thematic analysis, and also to demonstrate rigour in the research, a proper recording system is essential.

Currently, digital voice recorders are probably the most widely used systems, although in the past varieties of tape recorders were used. It is important to ensure confidentiality in the recordings. One aspect of this is suggesting to respondents that they should try to avoid mentioning anyone by name but instead refer to their relationship or job role. You will point out that, in any case, you will replace any names that are spoken with a pseudonym.

Consent to recording needs to be an explicit part of the participant consent process. However, it is not necessary, once consent is given, for the recording apparatus to be visible and potentially distracting. I have found it helpful, once consent is given, to put the microphone under a book or magazine on a coffee table. This may serve a dual function in also preventing the apparatus from falling off the table.

In order to ensure that recordings do not get confused with each other, I find it helpful to speak at the start of the recording (before the session starts) giving a few essential identifiers. I would not include the name of the person interviewed, as an extra safeguard in case the recording fell into the wrong hands. A precise date and, if necessary, a location or time will be sufficient to ensure that you know which tape it is when you compare it with your diary. In this way the list of who is interviewed, and the content of what they said, are kept separate at all times even though you, as the researcher, can connect these. You should also create a table of names and dates of interviews or focus group sessions, separate from the transcripts. An alternative is to speak a number at the start of the recording, and to have a separate table or diary entry indicating to which session the number refers. Management of transcripts will be considered further in Chapter 5.

Points to note

Preparations for interviews and focus groups should include:

- aide-memoire questions;
- recording device;
- consent forms and participant information sheet;
- ID;
- fully charged mobile phone;
- emergency number.

Introducing interviews and focus groups

The purpose of interviews and focus groups within qualitative research is to gain data for analysis, not for therapeutic purposes for participants. Provided this is borne in mind, the common principles of social group work may be adapted as a helpful guide to facilitating the process. Basic principles for effective semi-structured interviews and focus groups may be developed readily from social work skills in working with individuals and groups. I find it particularly helpful to use social work texts relating to the interactionist model of the late Bill Schwartz, such as that by Lawrence Shulman (2009).

There are a number of points which you may wish to bring across during the interview or focus group session, which are discussed below. Apart from the logic of introductions and stating purpose at the start, the sequence of points to be made is not rigid, although you will probably want to consider them all in some form for most qualitative studies. In a focus group session you probably want to prepare an opening 'contracting' statement that engages the group and which covers most, if not all, of the points below. In both interviews and focus groups you may want to make comment in relation to these issues at various points during the session.

It is important to have some sort of introduction and that people have an opportunity to give the name by which they wish to be called. Some older people, for example, might prefer to be addressed by their family name rather than their first name. In a focus group session it is usual to start with an introduction in order to help people relax. In some situations you may wish to have an ice-breaker exercise. However, I would urge caution in the use of ice-breaker exercises. They can seem artificial and become counterproductive in some contexts. The key is to reflect, through tuning in, on the type of people attending, the topic of concern and the emotional climate that you want to create. It is probably better to think of aiming towards a 'relaxed working environment' rather than something too light-hearted for most studies.

The interview or focus group needs to begin after some introductions with a clear statement about the purpose of the session. This is crucial to setting the tone of the session and it is well worth investing time in planning the wording carefully, even if you plan to express it in a relaxed manner. This brief explanation of purpose sets the tone for the session, and will influence what follows.

The discussion is to be comfortable and generally enjoyable for participants as they share their experiences, ideas and perceptions. You may wish to refer to the benefit that you hope that participating will bring to the respondent(s). This will normally be in relation to the topic of the session, for example, an opportunity to reflect on these issues.

You may wish to say that there are no 'right' or 'wrong' answers, and that what you want is to hear their ideas, and that your probing questions will be to clarify their ideas and not to force them to say something different. It needs to be clarified in a focus group that disagreement is acceptable, and that there is no pressure to achieve a consensus. You could say that you expect group members to influence each other and discuss topics, with the words of one sparking off new ideas in another.

In an interview or focus group you will want to clarify your role as facilitating the person or people to explore and express their views and experiences. In a focus group you may find it helpful to explain near the start that you are likely to be quieter than they might expect because – once you have outlined the topics of interest – your main interest is to hear their way of understanding and perceive their issues.

You should, as part of the introductory process, address any particular obstacles to the interview or focus group session. There may be some recent personal or community event which makes proceeding with the session impossible or inappropriate. At a lower level, there may be some particular issue in the news or in the person's family which impacts on the interview or some topical aspect of the organisation or services which impinges on the agenda of the focus group. It is worthwhile to think carefully and sometimes acknowledge such things so as to 'clear the air' or make it 'legitimate' as an aspect of the discussion.

You will need to address the issue of confidentiality in the early stage of an interview or focus group, regardless of whether you have obtained written consent in advance. In a focus group you need to address from the perspective of seeking to establish some 'ground rules' about confidentiality regarding what other participants have said.

Example – Contracting for a focus group session

Introduce people as necessary. Thank people for coming and confirm their preferred style of address. [CLARIFYING PURPOSE] The focus of this study is risk and decision making regarding the long-term care of older people. I am interested in: the factors considered by health and social care staff undertaking assessments and how you make judgements about who needs institutional care; the planning of home care; how you communicate concerns to patients or clients and other professionals; and the concepts that you use. [CONNECTING WITH MEMBERS' INTERESTS] I hope that this session will be an interesting and useful time for you to discuss issues relating to decision making regarding community care of older people. [PROCESS] I will guide the discussion, but I am happy to follow interesting ideas that you raise. I hope and expect that your ideas will stimulate further discussion. [LEGITIMISING VARIETY OF OPINION] I am not seeking a consensus in the group, so please feel free to disagree with each other, or with me! I am not here to assess you for 'right' or 'wrong' answers, and I expect to have a range of views expressed. [ADDRESSING PARTICULAR OBSTACLES] I am running similar group sessions with other staff in this organisation, and in other organisations. It is important that you feel free to express your own opinions regardless of others in the group and without considering what members of other professions might say. [CONFIDENTIALITY] The research team will treat the material as confidential and will not be providing feedback on specific sessions, or individuals, to your employer unless something extremely untoward comes to light. We will provide a general feedback session on the overall findings in your organisation to which you will be invited. I must ask you to respect the confidence of others here, and not to disclose outside what is discussed here in a way that identifies anyone. Please give specific examples but, if possible, avoid using the names of patients or clients. It is more helpful if you use job titles to refer to colleagues. In any event, I will be changing any names mentioned to preserve confidentiality. [RECORDING] I would like to record the session if you are agreeable, because it would be very difficult for me to make sufficiently detailed notes. The recording will be typed up and anonymised so that the material cannot be traced to a particular individual or (as far as possible) to the Trust. If you say something that you would like to have erased, just tell me and I will do so. In order to make the typist's task easier, please speak clearly. [CLARIFYING MY ROLE] You will find that I do not engage

⟶

in the discussion as much as you might expect, because I want to hear your views. I may ask about things that you think I should already know, because I want to understand how you see the issue or topic. I may challenge you or play 'devil's advocate' in order to explore interesting ideas, but that does not mean that I disagree! [INVITING ENGAGEMENT] Do you have any questions or comments? [OUTLINING THE TOPICS TO BEGIN THE DISCUSSION] There are five main areas for discussion: I would like to begin with a general question:

(Adapted from Taylor, 2006b)

Points to note

At the start of interviews and focus groups, you should cover:

- introductions and forms of address;
- health and safety issues including fire exits;
- comfort issues including toilets and mobile phone use;
- purpose of the study;
- outline of the process of the session;
- addressing particular obstacles;
- confidentiality issues;
- recording – consent;
- explain facilitator's role.

General conduct of the session

The general shape of the interview or focus group session will be for the interviewer to open each part of the discussion with the grand tour question or topic. You are likely to have between about five and ten topics or question areas related to your central research topic. This opens the way for an the interviewee or focus group member to say whatever they want on the topic area according to how they conceptualise the issues. When the interviewee or focus group members seem to have said all they want to say, you might follow up with some prompts within that topic area before moving on to the next topic. The prompts are a way of fleshing out aspects that have not been raised during the open discussion, or exploring them further. Your set of prompts may develop as the series of interviews or focus group sessions progresses, although you would not change your overarching structure of grand tour questions.

In a grounded theory study it is permissible to use material from a previous interview or focus group in an explicit way to inform a subsequent interview or focus group. Naturally, you would begin with open questions on each topic. You might, however, follow up within a particular topic with prompts such as: 'In a previous focus group a respondent said X. What do you think of that? Does it ring true for you? Does that relate to your experience? How might this be different from your experience?' If you were to use this approach, you could describe your method as 'thematic analysis drawing on elements of grounded theory'.

Use of qualitative methods within service evaluation and audit

Qualitative methods might be used within service evaluation and professional audit to illustrate quantitative data. In principle, service evaluations and audit are not research by definition in terms of governance. However, putting open questions into a survey instrument can add richness to the data gathered.

Example – Qualitative comments illustrating quantitative data

Reasons for considering leaving the job as a home carer:

1. Unsociable hours (30 per cent)

2. Lack of management support (20 per cent)

3. Workload (17 per cent)

4. Lack of client appreciation (13 per cent)

E.g. Theme 2: Lack of management support

'See your line manager at Christmas to get your diary and that's it!' (Respondent E)

'I'm quite happy with the general set up [for supervision] knowing that if I have a problem it can be sorted on the telephone [to my supervisor].' (Respondent B)

'Supervision – don't have any. I just ring if I have a problem.' (Respondent D)

(Adapted from a service evaluation in Fleming and Taylor, 2007)

Practical conduct of interviews and focus groups

The essence of conducting an interview or focus group session has many similarities with social work interviewing or social group work, except that the focus is on gathering data and not on helping the individual. The standard social work skills of clarifying, conveying empathy, reflecting, challenging with contradictory facts and partialising are all useful. Language should be straightforward for the individual or group members to understand. It is important to avoid ambiguity in what you say, an aspect where piloting is particularly helpful. Your contribution in terms of the main grand tour questions should be carefully rehearsed, not to make it stilted but in order to ensure that the wording is unambiguous and concise.

Although the engagement of service users as co-researchers is beyond the scope of the target audience for this book, we should mention this as a valuable direction for the quality of research, when well thought out. There are various examples of engaging service users in co-conducting focus groups (e.g. Begley et al., 2012).

Activity

- Working with a partner, identify a question about client perceptions of a social care service.
- Work together to create three broad question areas regarding the client's perceptions.
- Shape two specific questions under each broad question area.
- Role-play asking these questions as if it were a qualitative interview regarding user perceptions of the service.
- Debrief and discuss the experience.
- Swap roles and role-play using the same questions.

Summary

- The essential purpose of interviews and focus groups within qualitative research is to gather data about people's experiences, perceptions, views and understandings of their life experiences.
- Focus groups give the added dynamic of interaction between respondents compared to interviews which can spark off new ideas in an interesting and useful way.
- Interviews and focus groups need careful preparation in terms of place, timing and an aide-memoire to guide the questioning.
- The social work skills of tuning in and contracting for interviews and group work can readily be adapted to qualitative data gathering, bearing in mind the different purpose.
- The conduct of focus groups and interviews can draw on essential social work skills such as clarifying, conveying empathy and challenge.

Further reading

Morgan, DL (1998) *The Focus Group Guidebook*. Thousand Oaks, CA: Sage.

This is a well-known practical book on conducting focus groups.

Ritchie, J and Lewis, J (2006) *Qualitative Research Practice: A Guide for Social Science Students and Researchers*. London: Sage.

This thorough textbook is good on the philosophy of 'knowing' and on the generalisability of qualitative research.

Silverman, D (2011) *Qualitative Research*. London: Sage.

This textbook is a classic by a well-established pioneer of qualitative research.

Stewart, DW and Shamdasani, PN (1990) *Focus Groups Theory and Practice, Vol. 20,* Applied Social Research Methods Series. Thousand Oaks, CA: Sage.

This is a useful textbook on the practice of projects using focus group.

5: Qualitative Data Analysis

Introduction

The focus of this chapter is on basic thematic analysis, which underpins all qualitative data analysis. This is generally appropriate for master's and final year undergraduate degree level research, audit and service evaluation projects undertaken on qualifying and post-qualifying social work courses of study. Whilst we focus on manual approaches to analysis, the potential of computer-assisted qualitative data analysis for larger projects is also considered. Consideration of particular approaches to qualitative analysis (such as grounded theory, interpretative phenomenological analysis, discourse analysis, ethnography, etc.) is beyond the scope of this book. We do, however, draw on some elements of grounded theory such as the concept of *saturation* in sampling and bringing forward ideas from previously gathered data.

The essence of qualitative research is to create a conceptualisation of the lived reality for respondents. The focus is on their experiences, the meanings that they ascribe to events and their perceptions of these. We are seeking an understanding that is generalisable in terms of being useful for understanding in a general sense what is typically happening for people in this situation: 'Analysis is about the representation... of social phenomena... We create accounts of social life and in doing so we construct versions of the social worlds and the social actors that we observe' (Coffey and Atkinson, 1998, p108).

This chapter focuses on the essentials of thematic analysis of qualitative data. In one form or another, the principles and practices included here underpin analysis in the various qualitative designs, such as grounded theory, interpretative phenomenological analysis, discourse analysis, etc. This book focuses on the essentials of small-scale projects suited to our readership. Data from interviews and focus groups is typically used for qualitative analysis. We consider interviews and focus groups as data-gathering methods, rather than as defining the whole of the method. The analysis is also part of the 'method', and it is core thematic analysis that is being considered here.

Schools of thought on qualitative methods differ at some points in the description that follows, and for PhD students more sophisticated approaches linked to particular qualitative approaches, such as grounded theory, interpretative phenomenological analysis, etc. are more appropriate (cf. Starks and Trinidad, 2007). Some qualitative methods, such as ethnography, move the balance more towards observation, rather than relying exclusively on the analysis of words. Other methods, such as discourse analysis, may include oral, written and other forms of recorded narrative as data within one cohesive analysis. Nonetheless, an understanding of underlying meanings, as in basic thematic analysis, underpins these qualitative approaches also.

As in other chapters, we use the language of 'research methods' which may be used within projects which may be deemed to be either research, professional audit or service evaluation for governance purposes. A 'blank box' following a prompt within a survey, such as in many service evaluations and professional audits, may be regarded as gathering qualitative data. However, it will be apparent that the lack of interaction to prompt and explore perceptions and experiences will limit the richness of data available for analysis compared to qualitative research per se.

Essentials of qualitative analysis

Qualitative research begins from developing a research topic of interest. This should not be called a hypothesis as it is not going to be tested. Rather it is a topic for exploration. Any research is to create an original, generalisable understanding that fills a gap in human knowledge. The primary justification for qualitative research is that the experience or situation is so unclear or ill-defined that we do not have concepts to describe and discuss it. Once we have a model, a theory or concept then a quantitative method can be used to measure or count the prevalence of the construct within some group of people (the 'population' to which it is generalisable).

The qualitative data is collected, transcribed and then coded in terms of meaning. Data may be words, sentences or paragraphs. Coding in units of short paragraphs is often most appropriate for social work projects that gather qualitative data using focus groups and interviews. Bear in mind that the allocation of sentences into paragraphs is really at the discretion of the person doing the transcription. When people speak they do not indicate where paragraphs begin and end. So during the transcription process it is helpful to be making the paragraph breaks at the most natural place where the essential idea or focus changes.

An essential principle of qualitative analysis is immersion in the data, coding each item according to its essential meaning. Ideally, new data is coded continuously as it is gathered. Themes are drawn out as data accumulates, changing rapidly at first. The themes or categories are the drawing together of the basic level codes applied to clusters of sentences.

A key skill is to reflect continuously on the material, comparing new material with what has been gathered already, and with the codes and themes emerging. Gradually, the number of new themes emerging slows down, and the number of refinements to themes reduces. This is known as 'saturation', a concept drawn from grounded theory (Evans, 2013). In principle, the logical way to define a sufficient sample for qualitative research is when saturation is reached. The number of interviews or focus groups required for this will depend on the breadth and depth of the topic being considered. For further discussion see Chapter 3.

You could view this qualitative analysis as a process where the researcher's experience of the data is transformed through familiarisation with the data and reflection on its meaning into the extraction of key concepts. These concepts are then tested against each other to look for patterns and how well they do or do not fit with other themes.

Qualitative analysis might be described as *analytic induction* or *grounded creativity*. It is a journey of discovery. Compared with quantitative studies there is prolonged contact with respondents, and the aim is to gain a holistic view of their context. The aim is to draw out themes while retaining the original format of the data (the speech) to illustrate each theme. The essence of qualitative analysis is to understand the sort of meaning that respondents attribute to their experiences, and the concepts that they use to think and talk about them.

Data management and transcription

When you come to undertake the analysis, the value of the detailed transcripts of respondents will become apparent. Chapter 4 included material on how to record data. In order to demonstrate that your analysis is based on a wide range of respondents, it is customary to provide some ascription against each quotation used. These ascriptions might indicate a respondent's sex, age, job title or service need, etc. as appropriate to the focus of the study. Care will need to be taken to ensure that the amount of detail does not breach confidentiality. Geographical ascription requires particular caution. If you are conducting interviews it will be readily apparent who spoke which words, and you will be able to ascribe the quotations readily. For focus group discussions, it is rarely possible to identify what each member said and, in keeping with the philosophy of qualitative research, each focus group is regarded as a homogeneous group for the purposes of the research. Each group can be given a descriptor such as geographical location or professional group. If there is more than one group of a particular type you could label them A, B, C, etc., for example, (social workers, group A), (social workers, group B).

The recorded data needs to be transcribed into written form. There is an advantage in the main researcher doing this, as you are more likely to be able to guess what is being said if any words are unclear. However, with a large data set this becomes impossible and someone else may undertake the transcription. In this case, the person who conducted the interview or focus group will need to check the transcripts for accuracy, as soon after the event as possible. The transcript for an hour of interview is likely to be about 20 pages long, and will probably take about a day to transcribe from the recording.

Coding and drawing out themes

The description of qualitative data analysis that follows is designed for generic thematic analysis projects at master's degree level. It draws particularly on grounded theory. This is the most common, foundational approach. Analysis starts by looking at the first response from the first respondent and working onwards from there. For a grounded theory study it is emphasised that theoretical material should not be used unless and until the relevant topic emerges from the data. This does not mean that you cannot do any preliminary reading. Indeed, if you did not tune in to sensitise yourself to a range of possible responses you are unlikely to be a very effective researcher. However, you must consciously endeavour to avoid bias towards any particular theoretical way of understanding the data. Within an interpretative phenomenological approach it is permissible to 'test out' a theoretical construct that has been included from the start of the study design, although it should be noted that this is unusual amongst qualitative approaches.

The first statement by a respondent is considered for its essential meaning and a code word or phrase is ascribed to it. The next utterance by a respondent is then treated the same way, and so on. This analysis may be at the level of words, sentences or paragraphs. For our purposes, short paragraphs are probably most useful in capturing meaning without getting into minutiae of linguistic analysis. Note that the length of paragraphs is determined by (1) a statement by another speaker, whether the interviewer or a person in the focus group; and (2) the person transcribing the recorded data into written form, as we do not usually indicate paragraph length in speech. Normally, the paragraphs relating to a particular code are copied and pasted into a new document, or section of a document, labelled with that code. The use of qualitative data analysis software for this purpose is discussed below.

As this coding process develops, the 'shape' of the codes, in terms of what they include or refer to, will become clearer. The codes normally form a hierarchy or tree structure such that some codes are subdivided into sub-codes. By the end of coding the first transcript you should compile a table of operational definitions of the codes. This is a summary of what, so far, you mean by that code and what is included within it. This will have the same tree structure as the collection of quotes under each code. It is important to be as precise as possible in the wording of the codes so as to give a reasonable representation of what is included and what is not. An example of a coding schema is given below.

Example – A coding scheme for qualitative analysis

SAMPLE Codes (themes) in a study of perceptions of care risks regarding decision making about long-term care of older people, with operational definitions.

1. *Client choice and consent* [The wishes, demands, preferences and choices of the client. NB refusing a service is coded under theme XXX as this presents more of an issue for the professional.]

    1.1. *Client capacity to choose and consent* [The capacity of the identified client to exercise choice, including uncertainty about this, action taken to ascertain capacity, the outcomes of such action, and actions when a person is deemed not to have capacity.] ‹LINKS TO theme: Taking risks›

    1.2. *Client self-awareness* (or lack of) [The level of awareness of the patient or client particularly relating to the problem or issue related to risk.]

    1.3. *Limits to client choice* [Factors that limit the choice that may be exercised by a client or patient] including: client refused a service [where a client or patient is refused a service that is desired by the client or patient] and age as a factor in determining services received [any situation where age is perceived as a factor in determining the level or type of service received].

    1.4. *Written consents* [The consent in writing by a client or patient (or person acting on behalf of a client or patient) to a course of action, inaction, treatment or care.]

    1.5. *Client involvement (or lack of) in decision making* [The involvement of the client in the decision making about some aspect of care including provision of services and admission to institutional care.]

$\longrightarrow$

2. *Family carer* [A member of the client's family who provides significant care for the client.]

    2.1. *Family carer choice or decision making* [The wishes, demands, preferences and choices of the family carer and involvement in decision making.]

    2.2. *Family carer needs, stress, etc.* [The aspects of the life of the family carer that are identified by the carer, the client, or a professional as requiring an intervention in order to provide a satisfactory quality of life, or to prevent failure of the caring arrangement although occasionally the needs of carers and client are considered more in a more balanced way.]

    2.3. *Family carer presence, capacity, strengths, abilities or roles* (and limitations to caring) [The strengths, abilities, capacity and role of the family carer in caring for the older person. This may be limited, for example, by the health of the family carer.] ‹LINKS to theme: Assessment of family carers›

3. *Presentation of client needs* [The way in which the needs of the client or patient are presented, seen from the perspective of the client or patient, carer, neighbours or society in general. Note also code 3.1 below on the professional perspective on the initial contact.]

    3.1. *Crisis context* of presentation of need for long-term care. [Where the client needs are presented in a crisis, including hospital admission.]

    3.2. *Abuse and suicide* [References to the abuse of a client or patient, whether physical, sexual, emotional or financial, or to the possibility of suicide. Note also separate theme: Use of procedures to protect vulnerable adults.]

    3.3. *Home circumstances needs* [Needs that arise from the condition or situation of the dwelling occupied by the client.]

    3.4. *Physical needs* (includes falling, difficulty in activities of daily living (ADLs), stroke, skin care, managing medication, etc.) [Physical needs of the client including those related to ill health, disablement and (dis)ability to undertake necessary functions of daily living including inadequate nutrition, managing medication, etc.]

    3.5. *Mental health needs* [Mental needs of the client including dementia and mental ill health. NB Distinct from client or patient choice and capacity to choose and ascertaining capacity to choose, coded under theme: Client choice and consent.]

    3.6. *Financial needs* [Discussion of the financial circumstances of the client.]

    3.7. *Social needs* [The needs of the client to be part of society such as through involvement in a church, club or other group. This is coded separately from other social needs such as: contact with neighbours and fear of living alone.]

    3.8. *Night care needs* [The needs of the client for care of any sort during the night, usually relating to the ability of a family carer to provide this or the possibility or otherwise of such a service being provided by the public purse.]

(from study reported in Taylor and Donnelly, 2006a)

These operational definitions of codes are then continuously updated as you continue coding the transcripts. You may add notes about topics that do not belong within that code, and indicate where they are coded. This signposting is particularly valuable for a larger-scale study. As the coding proceeds, you can write 'memos' to yourself, such as insights into how codes relate to each other and how codes relate to theoretical concepts and previous studies. Again, it is good to be as precise as possible in writing memos, so as to indicate what you are referring to unambiguously. The breadth of understanding and application should be deliberate. You may wish to flag particular words for further reflection and refinement later.

Example – Coded paragraphs form a theme

From interviews about 'risks to elderly people' short paragraphs were grouped under the following code labels:

- knowing someone who was burgled;

- less respect from local youth;

- concern at crime rate;

- fear of assault (during burglary or on the street);

- not wanting to appear vulnerable (e.g. as a reason for refusing a stair rail at the front door).

These codes were brought together under a theme: *Fear of burglary and assault.*

(cf. Taylor and Donnelly, 2006a)

The essence of qualitative analysis involves a 'grounded creativity' in shaping a new understanding of the data. Insight and reflection are required in order to draw out insightful and interesting themes with wider application. The process of qualitative research feels very different from a quantitative study. The ongoing, iterative process is very apparent, rather than the clear stages of the administration of data gathering then analysis that is common in a survey. Some good advice is to start writing straight away! Write down your reflections as you go along, right from the first interview or focus group. What themes seem to be important to you with your growing overview of the understandings of respondents? What are people taking for granted, as much as speaking? How do participants think, feel and act in the life processes that form the focus of the study? What are the conditions and consequences of these processes? Can you make connections between things that are said?

It can also be useful to write a memo on how the coding develops. This can be valuable for reflection and to develop your transferable learning about the research process.

Example – Themes forming a model in qualitative research

From interviews about 'risks to elderly people', four major themes were identified:

- physical needs do not equate to experienced need for admission to care home;

- admission often arises in a crisis, e.g. admitted to hospital and afraid to return home;

- fear of burglary and assault;

- fear of falling.

These themes form elements of a model: *Older person living along no longer has confidence to continue doing so.*

(Taylor and Donnelly, 2006a)

Paragraphs are coded, and codes are grouped into themes. With a substantial study elements of a model or theoretical conceptualisation become apparent. A theoretical model is a way of understanding the main components of a situation, with some concept of how the parts relate to each other in the processes of life. A key skill is getting the correct 'focal length' (Boyatzis, 1998). You do not want to become immersed in the minutiae of speech (unless you are studying linguistic aspects), nor do you want to be so far removed that you merely note what is happening in terms of existing sociological constructs.

Research summary

Creating elements of a model from qualitative data

Risk management systems and structures are developing rapidly within UK health and personal social services. However, the risk management strategies of organisations need to take into account the conceptual frameworks used by professionals. This grounded theory study used data from 19 focus groups and nine semi-structured interviews (99 staff in total) to explore perspectives on risk and decision making regarding the long-term care of older people. Focus group participants and interviewees comprised social workers, care managers, consultant

(Continued)

(Continued)

geriatricians, general medical practitioners, community nurses, occupational therapists, home care managers and hospital discharge support staff. Social work and health care professionals conceptualised risk and its management according to six paradigms that appeared to be in a state of reciprocal tension: (1) identifying and meeting needs; (2) minimising situational hazards; (3) protecting this individual and others; (4) balancing benefits and harms; (5) accounting for resources and priorities; and (6) wariness of lurking conflicts. Each conceptualisation of risk had its sphere of relevance and inconsistencies at the boundaries of this. Professionals seemed to use the conceptualisation that was most appropriate for the immediate situation, changing to another conceptualisation when this was more useful. The effective translation into practice of risk management strategies needs to address the complex and often contradictory issues facing health and social services professionals.

(Taylor, 2006)

Computer-assisted qualitative data analysis

There is now a wide variety of computer software designed to support qualitative data analysis. These are very useful for managing large data sets, and for facilitating the labour-intensive aspects of qualitative analysis such as collating extracts of transcripts under each theme and code. A word of caution is in order, however, as none of those available is Microsoft or Apple. The commands are thus not as intuitive as most of us have become accustomed to, and you will need to allow time to learn in order to use them efficiently. The main software packages available include:

- Recommended to find, display and retrieve coded data:
  - *HyperQal2, Kwalitan, QUALPRO, Ethnograph*
- Recommended also for organising and sorting text:
  - *AskSam, FolioVIEWS, Tabletop, MAX*
- Recommended also for theory generation:
  - *AQAD, HyperRESEARCH, Nvivo*
- Recommended for theory 'testing':
  - *Atlas-ti, MECA, SemNet.*

(cf. Fetterman, 1998)

In general, software for qualitative analysis assists in seeing the structure of themes and codes that are being developed. They can facilitate the retrieval of the material that has been coded. Generally they facilitate coding by line, by sentence or by paragraph, and also multiple coding, i.e. coding an extract to more than one code. The best systems also facilitate 'pruning' a group of extracts from one code and 'grafting' it onto another. Typically they also facilitate searching for particular words in the text or the codes.

Generally, computer software can improve the quality of qualitative analysis by reducing the effects of fatigue and by making large data sets more manageable. Data is readily manipulated once on the system. Creating a visual 'tree' of codes is perhaps one of the most useful features in terms of actually facilitating the coding (di Gregorio, 2000) quite apart from their usefulness in managing the data set efficiently. Software packages support a wide range of types of thematic analysis. On the negative side, do not expect a software package to 'do the analysis for you' in the way that IBM SPSS might carry out a statistical test. The coding still remains in your own hands. The software is a tool, not a method of analysis. Be wary of getting carried away with the ease of the process and creating too many codes. Check before committing yourself to a particular software package that your transcripts can be easily imported, and that the analysis can be readily exported to whatever system you are using for your report. Systems are generally compatible with Microsoft Word, but compatibility with Apple is a work in progress.

It is, of course, possible to use standard word processing software for qualitative data analysis. Ensure that you make a second (electronic) copy of each transcript: one for reference and one to cut and paste. It is often helpful to number the lines of the transcript (in Word use 'page layout'/'line numbering' in the tabs at the top of the screen). It is possible to add a column to record the codes. The 'comment' feature in 'track changes' may be used to write memos to yourself, quite apart from any use in relation to a second coder. If you create a new page for each theme as it develops you will need to create a new page each time you create a new theme. Alternatively you can work with one long document divided into themes and codes. You can use 'page break' (in the 'insert' tab) to create a new page for each theme. You can then use 'control'/'page down' on the keyboard to move quickly from one theme to another. You can use 'find' within the 'home' tab to locate particular words that you know that you have coded before or used as a coding label.

Use of theory within qualitative analysis

Once the data is coded into categories linked to overarching themes, the data should be interpreted in relation to theoretical ideas from the literature review. It is important to ensure that existing theory sensitises the researcher rather than blinkers you in the analysis. Most qualitative models aim to start with a *tabula rasa*, meaning that the analysis is not forced into any predefined theoretical structure. This does not mean that the researcher needs to have an empty mind or conduct no preliminary reading of literature! Such a person would not be capable of undertaking qualitative research or being sensitive to the comments of respondents. Starting with a *'blank slate'* means that the analysis commences with coding the first line of the first transcript onto a blank page. The analysis works forward from there with successive paragraphs and transcripts. The structure of codes thus comes from the data rather than from any preconceived theoretical structure. (The main exception is interpretative phenomenological analysis where it is permissible to 'test out' a theoretical model as part of the data collection and analysis. This is beyond the scope of this book and the interested reader is referred to Starks and Trinidad, 2007.) 'Data are there to think with and to think about… We should bring to them the full range of intellectual resources, derived from theoretical perspectives, substantive traditions, research literature, and other sources' (Coffey and Atkinson, 1998, p153).

For all qualitative studies, it is important to be clear what material is from your own study as distinct from findings, theories or conclusions from other studies. For this reason, reports on qualitative studies conducted as part of examined academic programmes tend to make presentation of the data and the possible connections with existing theoretical material more distinct than in some other examples.

The relating of your data to the existing literature can take place in the discussion section, as in any small-scale project involving any methodology. In a qualitative study the emphasis is more on how the findings relate to existing theory. By contrast, a typical survey is likely to be related in the discussion section with a wider range of types of literature and other empirical findings. It is also possible to have a more dynamic interplay between the findings and existing theory: 'We use ideas in the literature in order to develop perspectives on our own data, drawing out comparisons, analogies and metaphors… We write narratives as well as analyse them…' (Coffey and Atkinson, 1998, p110).

Creating theory and models

A good qualitative study aims to create a new theoretical or conceptual understanding of the experiences or conceptualisation of some group of people. It is not a statistical model, but rather a theoretical model which aims to be useful to provide a working understanding of these types of situations or processes. Creating a theoretical understanding may be rather ambitious for a project at undergraduate or master's degree level, but with a tight scope and saturation sampling there are possibilities. Normally what is achieved is a range of themes that illustrate the topic, as opposed to demonstrating typical mechanisms or processes. An example of a theoretical model derived from qualitative research is given below, and other examples for the interested reader are in Beart et al. (2004), Taylor (2006b) and Taylor and Donnelly (2006a; 2006b).

Example – Steps in identity transformation for recovery of a heroin addict

1. STEP 1 Resolving to stop

2. STEP 2 Breaking away from addiction

3. STEP 3 Staying abstinent

4. STEP 4 Becoming and being ordinary

Example of codes within themes:

Within Step 4: Becoming and being ordinary:

a. Identity transformation

b. Emergent identity – reverting to unspoilt identity – extending identity

c. Surmounting the barriers to change

d. Relationships with addicts, non-addicts – speech nuances

e. Stabilisation of identity, perspective and relationships

f. Social commitments – drug-related experiences that confirm identity change

(Biernacki, 1986)

A good theory or model has a clear focus and is coherent and useful in understanding some aspect of social life. Each of the elements is supported by study data, with no gaps. A robust theory will stand the test of time, but will also be modifiable (Charmaz, 2006). A theory derived from qualitative research provides a way of understanding typical social mechanisms and processes.

Reflection

Qualitative research is inherently subjective. The researcher gathering rich, qualitative data needs to interact with the people who are the source of data as an essential part of the process. There is, of course, the possibility of bias due to preconceived ideas of the researcher or the perceptions of the respondents about the researcher. Respondents may be inclined to say what they think the researcher wants to hear, depending on the perceived role, affiliation or status of the researcher. There is the possibility of bias from the researcher in the analysis, and in the frame of reference or knowledge base that is used.

An important dimension of qualitative research to address this subjectivity is to ensure that there is a reflective process built in to the study. Quite apart from the emphasis within the social work profession on reflection as a key aspect of learning to apply theory to practice, qualitative research has always emphasised reflexivity as a research process. It is important that the researcher reflects on his own role, assumptions and frame of reference. An awareness of how he might be perceived can enable the researcher to address this during the interviews or focus groups. Reflexivity is regarded as an essential component of good qualitative research. For other dimensions of quality in qualitative research the interested reader is referred to Drisko (1997).

Points to note

It is important to remember the following when seeking quality in qualitative analysis:

- sound rationale for the study;
- focus on 'natural' settings;
- appropriate data-gathering tools for rich data;
- quotations illustrate range of respondent perspectives;
- findings are well-grounded in the data;
- effective linking to existing theory;
- demonstrates reflexivity;
- develops a coherent, useful theoretical understanding.

Summary

This chapter has focused on:

- the analysis of qualitative research, and on the analysis of qualitative data in audit and service evaluation projects derived from interviews and focus groups, with a focus on the basic thematic analysis which underpins all qualitative data analysis;
- the practicalities of data management, transcription, coding and developing themes;
- helping you to develop a feel for the iterative, incremental process involved in the organisation, classification and reduction of data to a manageable format to facilitate meaningful and insightful analysis;
- manual approaches to analysis, and also the potential of computer-assisted qualitative data analysis for larger projects;
- the use of theory within qualitative analysis;
- reflection as an essential component of qualitative research.

Further reading

Bazeley, P (2013) *Qualitative Data Analysis: Practical Strategies*. London: Sage.

This is a useful book on practical issues in analysis of qualitative data.

Boeije, H (2010) *Analysis in Qualitative Research*. London: Sage.

This is a useful book on analysis of qualitative data.

Boyatzis, RE (1998) *Transforming Qualitative Information: Thematic Analysis and Code Development*. Thousand Oaks, CA: Sage.

This is a good general textbook on analysis of qualitative data and is particularly insightful on the concept of 'focal length' in qualitative analysis.

Hogan, J, Dolan, P and Donnelly, P (2009) *Approaches to Qualitative Research: Theory and its Practical Application: A Guide for Dissertation Students*. Cork: Oak Tree Press.

This is a clearly written practical book for undergraduate and master's degree-level projects.

Charmaz, K (2006) *Constructing Grounded Theory*. New York: Sage.

This is a good textbook on grounded theory, but straightforward enough for application to general thematic analysis.

Ritchie, J and Lewis, J (2006) *Qualitative Research Practice: A Guide for Social Science Students and Researchers*. London: Sage.

This textbook is particularly good on the philosophy of 'knowing' and on the generalisability of qualitative research.

Silverman, D (2006) *Interpreting Qualitative Data* (3rd edition). New York: Sage.

This book by a pioneer of qualitative research provides a good outline of the essential elements of qualitative analysis.

6: Introduction to Quantitative Methods

Chapter aims

This chapter will:

- provide an overview of a number of quantitative methods relevant to social work research;
- discuss random controlled trials, quasi-experimental designs, pre-test and post-test designs, cohort studies, case-controlled studies and surveys;
- highlight distinct subsections and consider the main characteristics of the various approaches and demonstrate the different methods via examples from the author's research and those published within peer reviewed journals;
- consider the many nuances and distinctive characteristics of each of the designs, and highlight the key features of each of the quantitative methods.

Introduction

When social work research students first hear the term quantitative research methods they recoil in varying degrees of horror or dismay and assert quite quickly that this method is NOT for them. Over the years of teaching undergraduates and postgraduates it has become increasingly clear that many students choose what they see as the 'easier' option of a qualitative approach in research. However, when formulating their research ideas and plans they begin to acknowledge that one method is not necessarily 'easier' than another when collecting data and analysing the results.

However, it has also been heartening to see the shadow of doubt slowly dissipate as the pragmatic nature of the quantitative methods is explained. Likewise, it is always satisfying to witness how relatively easily the research students can grasp the quantitative method and operationalise it in social work research. Whilst most choose a survey method (described later on in this chapter) many students are increasingly opting for quasi-experimental and pre-/post-test designs, and are beginning to see the advantages of utilising such methods to enhance programme evaluations and add to the body of knowledge around what works best for their service user group and setting. This chapter will outline the various forms of quantitative methods used by social work postgraduate and undergraduate students in a variety of projects. It must be noted that the list is not exhaustive and there are other methods that can either be used alternatively or alongside the specific method described.

The typology of methods referred to in this chapter include the following:

- random controlled trials;
- quasi-experimental designs;
- pre-/post-test designs;
- cohort studies;
- case controls;
- survey methods.

Examples from recent undergraduate and postgraduate social work students alongside the author's own examples and external examples will be used to demonstrate each method.

Random controlled trials (RCTs)

RCTs are used to determine the effectiveness of an intervention (Newman, 2005). Traditionally, this method was used to gauge the efficacy of medical intervention, for example, the effectiveness of a specific drug in treating young men with depression. However, it is increasingly used to determine the effectiveness of psychosocial interventions which are relevant to social work (cognitive behavioural therapy (CBT), family therapy, reminiscence therapy, etc.).

Example – Random controlled trial

A multi-site, randomised controlled trial for children with abuse-related post-traumatic stress disorder (PTSD) symptoms.

Judith A Cohen, MD, Esther Deblinger, MD, Anthony P Mannarino, PhD, and Robert Steer, EdD. *Journal of the American Academy of Child Adolescent Psychiatry*. 2004 April, 43(4): 393–402.

$\longrightarrow$

Objective: To examine the differential efficacy of trauma-focused, cognitive behavioural therapy.

Trauma-focused CBT (TF-CBT) and child-centred therapy (CCT) for treating PTSD and related emotional and behavioural problems in children who have suffered sexual abuse.

Method: 229 children aged eight to 14 and their primary caretakers were randomly assigned to the above alternative treatments. These children had significant symptoms of PTSD with 89 per cent meeting full Diagnostic and Statistical Manual of Mental Disorders (DSM) IV PTSD diagnostic criteria.

There are a number of important facets of the RCT including:

A **null hypothesis** is used (this means that the researchers begin with the concept that there is no difference in outcomes between the two groups).

Randomisation of participants to specific treatment, control or waiting list control groups is viewed as the most important facet of the controlled trial. Randomisation aims to produce a random sample, from the population represented (for example, clients using a counselling service in a one-year period).

In other designs without randomisation, researchers may try to match people who are similar in the various groups to be researched but this is a difficult task and the outcomes at the end of the programme may be as a result of differences in participant characteristics at the beginning of the programme rather than as a result of the treatment. In order to avoid this, randomising the participants to the comparison groups receiving treatments ensures that they are fairly equal in terms of certain factors which may include age, gender, type of diagnosis, etc. The process ensures that all factors that might have an impact on results will be evenly distributed across the groups.

For the random assignment to be considered as truly random, a number of conditions must be met. Each person must have an equal chance of being assigned to each of the groups. For example, if there are two groups (A and B) and the researcher flips a coin to determine who is assigned to each group, then each person has a 50:50 chance of being assigned to either group.

In addition, each individual's chance of ending up in either group A or group B must be independent of the chances of the other individuals. For example, if we first divide the groups into male and female, then flip a coin within each group then it is certain that each group will either be comprised of female or male members. Each female is linked to the other in that group and the chances of being chosen are not independent of all members in the complete group of males and females. Of course, it is true that a random assignment does not guarantee that there is complete similarity between the groups and it might be the case that a few more females may be included in one group rather than the other. However, with a large enough sample this is less likely.

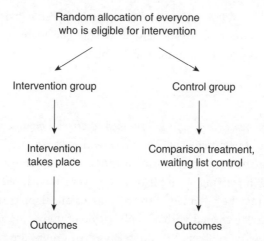

Figure 6.1 Random allocation in the research process

Randomisation is usually conducted via a computer-generated programme to avoid human error.

A **power calculation** ensures that the correct number of people have been recruited to the study to adequately test the research hypothesis and to achieve statistical significance in the results (Cohen, 1988).

A **control group** is also an important feature of RCTs. Members of a control group may either receive the intervention to be studied or receive something else – this may be referred to 'treatment as usual' or 'standard care'. For example, you might wish to consider the effectiveness of person-centred counselling for young women with mild depression. However, in social and health care research it is difficult to work within ethical guidelines when one of the groups is assigned to a control group that is not allocated any treatment in order to compare the results with those receiving the intervention.

However, in a lot of social care research where you are not comparing two interventions, the control group may be comprised of individuals who are on a waiting list (known as a waiting list control).

The group(s) of people being tested

The inclusion/exclusion criteria for the group is usually quite strict and, of course, relevant to the objectives of the RCT in question. There is usually a rigid specification of the characteristics that delimit the study population via the eligibility or inclusion criteria. For example, one could consider how effective family group conferencing is for young male and female offenders between the ages of 14 and 17 years. It may be further specified that the 'offending' characteristic would be related to those who had been convicted of a criminal offence. The age range ensures that adult offenders are not considered and it is also clear that the recruiting to sample is open to both male and females.

The intervention

The intervention is the type of treatment being used to effect a change in the group of people being researched. It should be noted that there may be more than one intervention used to provide a comparison for the outcomes treatment group. For example, a project could consider the effectiveness of CBT in treating a sample of young women with bulimia. As part of the RCT, one of the groups may be provided with CBT (as a standalone treatment) for bulimia, whilst another group may be treated with a combination of fluoxetine and CBT and a third group may be in receipt of person-centred counselling. All groups are tested before and after the intervention in order to assess which treatment is most effective.

Quasi-experimental designs

A quasi-experimental design differs from the RCT in one important aspect, that is it does not utilise random assignment to the treatment and control groups. However, the main purpose of the design is to determine whether the programme or intervention has the intended effect on the study participants. It is often more appropriate to use the quasi-experimental design in social work research due to practical and ethical reasons. It may not be feasible to randomly assign service users to particular groups (for example, it may only be possible to use a waiting list control and it is difficult to utilise random assignment in a situation where an individual may come off the waiting list at any given time).

Whilst random assignment is not associated with the quasi-experimental design, the method is used regularly to explore the effectiveness of interventions. Researchers try to overcome the possibility of bias in the results by trying to match the participants' characteristics in both groups prior to assignment to either group and by controlling for differences in the groups at the analysis stage.

Example – Quasi-experimental study

Campbell, A (2015) Interim report of ongoing study. A research evaluation of the well woman BACP-registered counselling programme for women.

The research is evaluating the outcomes of a BACP-registered well woman counselling programme via the CORE evaluation tool. It examines whether the counselling programme assists women to address global distress as measured by the CORE evaluation tool.

$\longrightarrow$

It was envisaged that from an average population of 95 participants, who were to be assessed to engage in the well woman programme over a 12-month period (based on the 95 assessed between 10 April and 11 April), 80 women were selected by the researchers on a rolling basis to participate in the quasi-experimental phase of the research study. In 2009, 61 women were on the waiting list for an average of six months and 55 women received counselling (15 women were categorised as semi-urgent and commenced counselling immediately).

Sample of 95 women anticipated to be assessed by well woman organisation over a 12-month period.

NO RANDOM ASSIGNMENT TO EACH GROUP

Intervention group   Control group
(n=40)   (n=40)

BASELINE ASSESSMENT

(using CORE tool)

Intervention   Waiting list control

OUTCOME ASSESSMENT

At three-month and six-month stages (or before the six-month stage if control group participant moves from the waiting list).

The selected intervention group (n = 40) were interviewed using the CORE tool prior to the commencement of counselling and subsequently followed up at three-month and six-month junctures. The control group (n = 40) was obtained from the waiting list, which fluctuated between 40–60 over a 12-month period. Members of the waiting list control were also interviewed using the CORE tool at the initial assessment and at three-month and six-month junctures. (Participants usually remained on the waiting list for between four and six months.) In cases where participants obtained a counselling place between the four- and six-month junctures, they were interviewed immediately prior to the commencement of the counselling programme.

Attrition rate in experimental and quasi-experimental designs

It should be noted that the attrition (drop out) rate was 20 per cent in the study described above and there are a number of ways suggested by authors to keep the attrition rate to a minimum when conducting quasi-experimental research. First, it is important to ensure the commitment of the study participants and make sure that participation in the first phase of the study (i.e. initial interviews) is not in any way a negative experience. Participants must also be informed that they will be interviewed on second and possibly third occasions and it must be made clear that this is necessary to gain the required outcomes. All the usual informed consent issues apply with assurance of confidentiality and anonymity but, again, at the informed consent stage it must be underlined that this is applicable to all stages of the research continuum. The researcher must also be available to answer any questions that arise between the interview junctures as participants often 'go away' and think of reasons not to participate further. Follow-up phone calls are useful to ensure that participants return and the value of their participation must be emphasised at this and other stages throughout the process and not just at the beginning interview. In addition, feedback could be provided from the initial phase and the researcher must provide a telephone number, mobile number and email address for ease of contact throughout the process. If you have established a website for the study, think about adding a chat thread to answer any questions (these may be answered by the researchers or other participants). Consistency is key to ensuring a strong follow up return and the commitment of the researcher is key to the success of the returner rate.

Pre-/post-test design

The pre-/post-test design does not use randomisation to groups or indeed make use of a control group for comparison purposes. The design simply researches a group of individuals before they receive a specific intervention or treatment and tests them again at the post intervention stage to determine whether there has been a change on the measures used between times one and two.

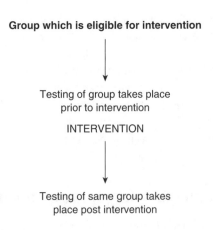

Group which is eligible for intervention

Testing of group takes place
prior to intervention

INTERVENTION

Testing of same group takes
place post intervention

Figure 6.2 Intervention

Example – Pre-/post-test design

Campbell, A (2004) A pre-/post-test evaluation of outcomes for drug-related offenders in a prison setting, Londonderry, University of Ulster.

Twenty-eight men over 18 years of age participated in a drug and alcohol awareness programme and counselling over a six-week period for three hours on a once-weekly basis. The method employed specific measures of attitudes to change and these were conducted with the participants at the pre-programme and post-programme stages.

Findings from the study were used to inform programme design and outcomes. The programme was changed to include a greater number of counselling sessions as the group therapy appeared not to be effective from the results of the stages of change questionnaire at the post-intervention stage. However, the results of the study were noted with extreme caution and were not generalisable to the remainder of the prison population in that prison and, indeed, other prisons in Northern Ireland and the rest of the UK. Nevertheless, it gave a tentative overview of outcomes and, alongside the views obtained from prisoners, it helped shape service provision for future programmes with offenders with drug and alcohol problems in that specific prison. It is possible that the positive effects gained from the programme for attitudes towards drug use may have changed due to the increased period of incarceration. In addition, prisoners could have been influenced by factors beyond the control of the researchers. For example, three of the group members joined a religious group which, they reported, had changed their views on drugs and alcohol.

Hawthorne effect

The effects of being observed are famously documented in the reporting of a study by Franke and Kaul (1978). A series of pre- and post-tests on worker productivity were considered in view of changes in environment. The Hawthorne effect underlined the need for control groups to validate the results of a pre- and post-test experiment.

Cohort studies

Cohort studies are used when researchers wish to know long-term outcomes for a specific subsection of the population using the same group of respondents over a long period of time. These are studies of the same group of people over that period or research on people who have been exposed to an event or specific lifestyle. For example, a study could consider the long-term outcomes for children who have been placed in two or more foster placements within a five-year period. There may be a control group but it is not an essential feature of the design and many cohort studies do not employ controls.

The primary feature of the cohort longitudinal study is that it usually moves forward in time and is essentially forward looking, taking note of the progression of the research participants at specific junctures in time. However, there may be some level of confusion over the time sequencing as cohort studies may choose a moment in the past life of the service user and follow up what has happened since that moment in time. This may at first appear retrospective in nature but if one remembers that the researchers are moving forward from that chosen moment then they are not looking back incrementally but flowing forward from the fixed point in time. In other words, individuals are identified at one point in time and followed up at a point further in the future.

These studies are considered weaker than random controlled trials or quasi-experimental designs because participants cannot be randomly allocated to the intervention (for example, residential or foster care). Therefore, it is difficult to say that any outcomes are a result of the specific factors. However, random selection of large groups across multiple sites will increase the generalisability of the findings.

Example – Cohort study

Currie, J and Widom, CS (2010) Long-term consequences of child abuse and neglect on adult economic wellbeing, *Child Maltreatment* 15(2), pp111–120.

Using a prospective cohort design, court-substantiated cases of childhood physical and sexual abuse and neglect during 1967–71 were matched with non-abused and non-neglected children and followed into adulthood (mean age 41). Outcome measures of economic status and productivity were assessed in 2003–4 (n = 807). Results indicate that adults with documented histories of childhood abuse and/or neglect have lower levels of education, employment and earnings, and fewer assets as adults, compared to matched control children. There is a 14 per cent gap between individuals with histories of abuse/neglect and controls in the probability of employment in middle age, controlling for background characteristics. Maltreatment appears to affect men and women differently, with larger effects for women than men. These new findings demonstrate that abused and neglected children experience large and enduring economic consequences.

Case control studies

In case control studies, study subjects are identified and enrolled as having, or not having, a given outcome. Researchers then look back into subjects' history (usually by reviewing records or relying on subjects' recall) to learn about their exposure status. Similar to the cohort study, time is an essential component of the study as case control studies consider facets of participants' lives and look retrospectively at what led to that point. The selection for case control is on the basis of an outcome characteristic and is compared to a control group that does not have this characteristic.

For example, one could make the comparison between a group of women who suffer from depression and a group of women without a diagnosis of depression and the experiences of both groups of women in relation to domestic violence throughout their lives. In this example, researchers have no control over the violence as the independent variable.

Example – Case control study

Marzano, L, Hawton, K, Rivlin, A and Fazel, S (2011) Psychosocial influences on prisoner suicide: A case control study of near lethal self-harm in women prisoners, *Social Science and Medicine*, 72, pp874–883.

The authors examined the psychosocial influences on female prisoner suicide by carrying out a study of near-lethal self-harm. They interviewed 60 women prisoners who had engaged in near-lethal self-harm (cases) and 60 others who had not engaged in near-lethal self harm in prison (controls) from all closed female prison establishments in England and Wales. The authors gathered data on socio-demographic and criminological factors, life events and childhood trauma, exposure to suicidal behaviours, contributory and precipitating factors for near-lethal self-harm, social support and psychological characteristics. Recent life events and past trauma, including different forms of childhood abuse, were significantly associated with near-lethal self-harm, as were a family history of suicide and high scores on measures of depression, aggression, impulsivity and hostility, and low levels of self-esteem and social support. The case control research findings underlined the importance of both individual and prison-related factors for suicide in custody, and the need for a comprehensive approach to suicide prevention in women's' prisons.

Surveys

Survey research is primarily utilised to describe what exists, whether it is events, behaviour or attitudes in a specific or general population. In social work, surveys are most often used to examine attitudes which are prevalent in relation to a specific subject area (for example, views on a specific social work service).

There are a number of different types of surveys:

1. Ad hoc surveys are usually employed to gather data on a one-off basis (McKenna et al., 2006), for example, gathering data via a survey of women people in relation to their views on a number of issues related to childcare, such as cost and accessibility (McColgan and Campbell, 2007). The survey was administered on one occasion to a total sample of over

1,920 women from a number chosen district council areas in cross-border regions between Ireland and Northern Ireland.

2. Longitudinal surveys are usually conducted over a long period of time, for example, the Life and Times Attitudes Surveys in Northern Ireland (1998–2013) or the British Social Attitudes Survey (1983–2014). The surveys referred to are carried out at regular intervals within the general population, or a subsection of the population, and include a core set of questions with additional questions added to reflect new and topical issues relevant to the objectives of the respective surveys. The surveys are used to monitor public attitudes towards ethnic minorities, health care and changing trends in social care (for example, the recent closure of a large number of residential places for older people in care homes within Northern Ireland).

Using survey methods in your research project

In general, survey methods are useful ways of gathering data for a specific purpose and most undergraduate and postgraduate social work research students tend to choose these methods to describe certain events, to look at changing trends over time or simply consider perceptions of respondents at a specific juncture in time on a one-off basis. If the sampling technique utilised is well planned and relevant to the objectives of the survey, then associations between variables may be examined and casual inferences may be explored.

Example – Survey

McColgan, M and Campbell, A (2007) A survey of childcare needs of women in the northwest of Ireland, Londonderry, University of Ulster.

This study examined the nature and extent of childcare services available in the northwest of Ireland in a defined period in 2006. It also identified the level of childcare provision for the 0–14 years age group throughout eight designated council districts and collated demographic data in relation to this specific age range.

Specifically, the survey, which was administered to women in the districts, examined their perceptions of the suitability and affordability of existing childcare provision. In addition, it ascertained and compared the perceptions of the success of existing childcare structures within the communities throughout each of the eight identified areas. Using established agency contacts from a previous consultation on determinants of mental health and emotional wellbeing (McColgan et al., 2003), a non-probability snowball sampling technique was employed, whereby four to 15 community representatives from each of the designated border areas administered approximately 40 questionnaires (see Chapter 3 for further discussion on snowball sampling techniques). The use of a snowball sampling method permitted the selection of community representatives who subsequently invited a number of individuals from their local communities to complete the questionnaire. Thus, as intended, the information gathered ascertained the view of the local populations in the council areas (Sarantakos, 2010).

$\longrightarrow$

Some 1,520 questionnaires were given out to the community gatekeepers, who in turn administered them to respondents in the local areas; 966 questionnaires were returned, giving a 63 per cent response rate.

The questionnaire comprised a number of open and closed questions, and also questions which were used to elicit likert data. These questions were used to establish demographic information such as area of residents, number of children in household, type of childcare used, frequency of use of childcare and perceptions of the success of the childcare arrangements, etc.

However, it is important to keep in mind that the data gathered does not account for the social context of meaning at the point in time at which the data is captured, the influences of outside factors such as respondents' health and wellbeing or the influence of recent familial or social events/experiences in their lives which may affect the responses to the questions. There is also the argument that surveys are concerned with measurement and that it is difficult to measure social phenomena at the core of social work interaction and intervention.

Survey research tools and question types

From the previous section it is clear that surveys may be used to gather data in a range of research projects. However, there is often confusion among students as regards:

1. Which type of data-gathering instrument or survey tools should be employed (for example, questionnaire, face-to-face survey, telephone survey or online survey).

2. The different types of questions which should be used within a survey method (for example, closed, open and Likert).

Face-to-face interviews

Face-to-face or telephone surveys may use either a standard questionnaire or interview guide which has a combination of closed, open and/or Likert-style questions. In this instance, researchers read out the questionnaire and record in a written format the answers as the person responds. The questionnaire used is in the same standardised format as the one administered for self-completion by the respondent, the difference being that the researcher is present to complete the survey questionnaire with the respondent either via phone or on a face-to-face basis. Students often confuse the face-to-face survey with the qualitative style open face-to-face interview. It is important to remember that the face-to-face survey uses a standardised set of questions which may elicit closed and open data, whilst the open face-to-face interview usually employs a qualitative interview guide which may be quasi-structured and will facilitate a gathering of more in-depth qualitative data and detailed tracts of prose information to allow for deeper meaning and contextual richness within the responses. This type of interview is usually recorded to analyse the themes in greater detail using a specific type of qualitative data analysis technique (see Chapter 5).

Online surveys

Online surveys are increasingly used to access greater numbers of people and a range of targeted populations across all areas of social science research. The advantages of the online survey include a reduced cost, a decrease in administering resources and the transfer of data from online survey software and questionnaires directly to statistical software packages. Free and easily accessible brands such as SurveyMonkey and SmartSurvey™ are being used by increasing numbers of students to access a plethora of targeted populations.

Example – Online survey employed as part of data collection in a recent PhD thesis

McFadden, P (2013) Resilience and burnout in child protection social work, University of Ulster PhD thesis.

The thesis employed a multi-method approach which included questionnaires and semi-structured interviews. When distributing the online questionnaires, the internal email system was used for convenience as principal investigators had access to distribution lists of employees. Workers were reassured that employers did not have access to the information on the questionnaires on an individual basis. Results were anonymous and individuals were not identified. This was clearly stipulated in writing. All social workers now use computers and email as part of their daily administrative tasks and, therefore, access to computers was not an issue. Principal Investigators across all six sites were confident that email correspondence and completion of the online questionnaires was within the social workers' range of skills.

The content of the 'data collection email' stated that consent had been given and that the participant was fully aware that completion of the survey was an admission of consent. Non-participants could simply disregard the email and decline consent to participate. On email, a web link enabled consenting participants direct access to the survey questionnaire which took 20–30 minutes to complete. The data results were converted from SmartSurvey software into a CSV file, which was compatible with SPSS 17 software for data analysis. Data was transferred for analysis using technology which is hacker safe and has a firewall installed. Data protection was also strictly adhered to. Furthermore, the software was Socket Security Layered (SSL) encrypted for enhanced security. The link to the questionnaire was: www.smart-survey.co.uk/v.asp?i=18175ykeeq.

SmartSurvey software had the added advantage of allowing participants increased confidentiality and privacy around participation in the study. Subjects could participate from home if they wished and in their own time.

(McFadden P, 2013, p125)

Types of data gathered by survey

The questionnaire can use a number of different question types to elicit different types of data responses and the three primary types of questions include closed, Likert and open questions.

Closed questions and responses

Closed questions usually employ a tick box format and are used to elicit yes/no answers. For example:

Do you think that social work students should have longer work placements? (Yes/No)

These types of closed questions are known as dichotomous as they usually only permit one of two responses. They are coded in a similar fashion to closed questions which elicit numeric data. Questions which engender numeric data may simply ask the person's age and this is recorded as single number, or may ask young service user respondents how many residential childcare placements they have experienced in the last two years. (Answer n = 3)

Or the question may ask the social work practitioner how many families on their current caseload have severe problems with drug and alcohol misuse? (Answer n = 21). The number is recorded as a single numeric coded entry and is analysed using various techniques which may be descriptive percentages or means (see Chapter 7 for further discussion of analysis of numeric data).

Closed questions are also used to gather demographic information such as marital status, accommodation type, job type, ethnic grouping, etc. The answers provided to these questions are obviously not numeric in format but are what are known as categorical responses, that is they are presented in a series of categories.

'What is your marital status?'

Categorised responses may be indicated as follows:

Single

Married

Living with partner

Widowed

Separated

Divorced

These are tick box answers and are analysed as categorical data (see Chapter 7 for further discussion).

Questions which gather Likert-style data

Questions can also be used to gauge the opinion of the respondents on certain subjects or areas. Consider, for example, the following question: 'How important do you think it is that you have teaching on drug and alcohol use in your social work degree prior to placement?' The answers provide Likert-style data beginning, for example, from least important or to most important:

1. Not at all important
2. Not important
3. Not quite sure
4. Important
5. Very important

The Likert-style question may have five to seven answer categories for the purpose of analysis.

Open questions

A series of open questions may be included within the questionnaire or face-to-face survey. Open questions elicit more detailed answers and usually ask the person to explain why they answered a previous closed question. For example, after asking social work students the question above about their views on the length of social work placements, one may continue with a question asking them to explain their answer:

'If you responded "yes" to the last question, can you tell us why think that social work placements should be extended?'

This type of question allows the respondent to provide a prose-type answer which is different from the standard tick box answer and, therefore, must be analysed in a different way using a thematic technique (see Chapter 7 for further discussion).

Summary

This chapter has focused on:

- a number of different quantitative design methods, and has looked at how a selection of them could be applied in practice using examples for postgraduate social work students;
- the survey method – covered in particular detail, as student social workers tend to employ this method in small-scale research projects with some opting for a pre-/post-design depending on the subject area;
- helping you to understand quantitative designs, as it should be acknowledged that there is room for a number of designs in small-scale and the more in-depth PhD study designs.

Further reading

Newman, T, Moseley, A, Tierney, S and Ellis, A (2005) *Evidence Based Social Work: A Guide for the Perplexed*. Dorset: Russell House Publishing.

Sarantakos, S (2012) *Social Research* (4th edition). Basingstoke: Palgrave Macmillan.

Coolican, H (2006) *Introduction to Research Methods in Psychology* (3rd edition). London: Hodder Education.

7: What Does It All Mean?
Exploring Quantitative Data Analysis

Chapter aims

This chapter will:

- consider a selection of quantitative data analysis techniques relevant to social work research projects;
- guide you through the inputting of data into a standardised computer package for data analysis;
- discuss the displaying of data in reports via charts, tables and histograms;
- examine a range of statistical tests commonly used in postgraduate and undergraduate social work research projects;
- focus on the importance of the concept of 'testing of significance'.

Introduction

There are a number of different types of quantitative data analysis, including meta-analysis, secondary analysis and primary analysis. Meta-analysis is the interrogation of data from a collection of research projects wherein the statistics produced by each project are analysed collectively to produce a rigorous analysis of the pooled data. For example, a researcher may wish to look at all available findings which consider the effectiveness of cognitive behavioural therapy for working with children who have been sexually abused (see MacDonald et al., 2012). Secondary data analysis refers to consideration of the data which has been collected from a primary source by another researcher. It is usually employed for the further interrogation of data from continuous longitudinal studies which have many subsections and which may be of interest to researchers from various backgrounds. The Northern Ireland Life and Times survey is an example of a continuous survey which was launched in October 1998 as a source of information for everyone interested in the social attitudes of people living in Northern Ireland. The survey aims to record the attitudes, values and beliefs of the people in Northern Ireland on a wide range of social policy issues (www.ark.ac.uk).

Primary data analysis is used by researchers who formulate specific research questions, plan and execute the research methodology and subsequently analyse the data that they have collected at one or more points in time. In a recent empirical project, two social work researchers wished to gauge the perceptions of academic tutors' views in relation to social work education in Northern Ireland. The researchers gathered data via a survey of tutors in two universities in the region and analysed the data collected from the questionnaires via a statistical package (SPSS). They investigated how respondents perceived the changes in social work education and the concomitant gaps in the university social work curriculum etc. The researchers looked at a number of associations between variables including the connection between time in post and perceptions of curriculum content and gender and attitude towards management and technocratic change in social work practice (Wilson and Campbell, 2013).

Sarantakos (2010) refers to stages of quantitative data analysis and provides a useful framework for the newly initiated as well as the seasoned researcher. The stages include:
(1) data preparation; (2) counting; (3) grouping; (4) relating; and 5) significance testing.

Data preparation involves coding the information collected from questionnaires, surveys, etc., editing the data, checking for missing data and, when computer statistical packages are used, compiling the database and entering the data from the research tools. A process of coding is then used through which responses are translated into numbers, for example:

What is your marital status?

1. Married

2. Co-habiting

3. Single

4. Separated

5. Divorced

6. Other

The digits 1–6 are known as values and the answer categories provided by the researcher are known as value labels. The values labels are set up as part of the original database and the value labels are inputted into the computer from each questionnaire/survey or other research tool. Counting or considering the frequency of occurrence may be completed on a manual basis or, more usually, via a statistical package. One function of a statistical package is to provide information on the number of times a certain answer is recorded or to convert that to a percentage of responses. For example, the researcher may have wished to consider the gender of the respondents or time in service. The package can provide information of the breakdown according to respondent gender or the proportion of respondents who have served a specific number of years in the same grade or social work role.

Grouping and presentation involves the representation of data in specific groups usually through tables or graphs. In presenting the findings, graphs might be used to depict the results from questions which show socio-historic data such as employment status in recent years.

Relating involves the consideration of relationships by using cross tabulations and statistical tests to determine the nature and strength of the relationships between different variables.

Points to note

What are variables and cases in quantitative data analysis?

When we talk about 'variables' in quantitative analysis, we are referring to the items most likely to be represented as questions within the questionnaire/survey or other tool and these are considered as separate units within the analysis process. For example, one question may look at a service user's view on feedback from assessment and the respondent may be asked to rate on a scale from 1–10. When creating the database, the researcher will consider this and other questions as separate variables whilst answers provided by respondents are known as cases.

Testing of significance

The definitive cut off points for statistical significance in results for the majority of statistical tests are $p < 0.05$ or $p < 0.01$.

The figure $p < 0.05$ means that there is less than a one in 20 chance that the result was accidental. The figure $p < 0.01$ means that there is less than a one in a 100 chance that the answer was accidental. There is a general consensus that an answer is statistically **significant** at $p < 0.05$ and **statistically highly significant** at $p < 0.001$ (less than one in a 1000 chance that the answer was accidental).

Most students using SPSS wrestle with the many functions, the meaning of tests and, above all, the interpretations of the results and what it means to their project. The preparation for data analysis is a daunting task in the formulation of the research study and may have an enormous impact on the choice not to employ a quantitative methodology.

The following section will discuss the inputting of data, displaying of quantitative data, the use of descriptive statistics, cross tabulations, chi-square statistics, the function of correlation techniques and the use of t-tests in quantitative projects. The chapter will use project examples from social work students and academic social work staff projects to illustrate the benefits of quantitative data analysis and also make reference to the common errors made by novice researchers.

Inputting the data into a computer package for statistical analysis

As previously noted, the most commonly used package for student statistical analysis is the SPSS package, although there are many more commercially available packages that are just as flexible or, indeed, provide in-depth analysis techniques for the more practised or adventurous student. These include Stata and Minitab (a comprehensive list of packages is available at: www.capterra.com/statistical-analysis-software/).

It is not within the remit of this chapter to take the reader through a step-by-step guide to the setting up of an SPSS file and a discussion of the inputting and cleaning of data. More comprehensive explanations may be found within Chapter 2 of Argryous, 2006 and part 2 of Pallant, 2013.

Variable types

Nominal or categorical variables have specific categories such as marital status or employment category. You can count but not order or measure nominal data.

An *ordinal variable* is similar to a categorical variable. The difference between the two is that there is a clear ordering of the categories. For example, a question may ask the person to rank level of agreement with a statement and the answers may be scaled from strongly disagree to disagree, unsure, agree and strongly agree.

Interval variables are variables whose central characteristic is that they can be measured along a continuum and they have a numerical value (for example, temperature measured in degrees Celsius or Fahrenheit). So the difference between 20°C and 30°C is the same as 30°C to 40°C. However, temperature measured in degrees Celsius or Fahrenheit is NOT a *ratio* variable.

Ratio variables are interval variables but with the added condition that 0 (zero) of the measurement indicates that there is none of that variable. So, temperature measured in degrees Celsius or Fahrenheit is not a ratio variable because 0°C does not mean there is no temperature. Examples of ratio variables include height, mass, distance and many more.

Displaying data – charts, graphs and tables

Basic descriptive data are most commonly presented by research students within reports/ projects through graphs (also known as charts) and tables. These provide a visual representation of the primary aspects of the distribution of data. Moreover, a graph may provide direct access to a summary of important demographic information by showing the number of times a certain answer is recorded, for example, n = 36 males or n = 67 females.

The graph will be constructed according to the type of data used: nominal, ordinal, interval or ratio scale. The most commonly used graphs are bar charts, pie charts, histograms and scatter graphs.

Points to note

- Before explaining the process of obtaining graphs/charts it is important to think about the purpose of displaying the information.
- Information on the graph should be instantly recognisable and need no further explanation other than the visual representation of data.
- Label axes and values clearly.
- Each graph should have a clear title (with the purpose of the graph being self-explanatory).
- Choose an appropriate scale as often the computer package will not do this or will display a misleading scale.
- For interval or ratio data, indicate the units of measurement.
- Show the total number of cases in the title or at the bottom of the graph.

Bar charts

To display data commonly referred to as nominal or categorical (for example, housing status or ethnicity), a bar chart may be constructed as in Figure 7.1, where the categories represent the values. In addition, you may show your data labels as percentages or numbers.

Example – How to obtain a bar chart in SPSS

- Choose Graphs > Legacy Dialog > Bar
- Click Simple > Summaries for groups of cases > Define
- Next, click Percentage or Number of Cases and move chosen variable into the category axis box and click OK
- Next, double click on the graph and choose Elements at the top of the graph
- Click on Show Data Labels to insert the percentage for each bar
- Click on Edit at the top of the graph and choose Select Chart to add a graph frame.

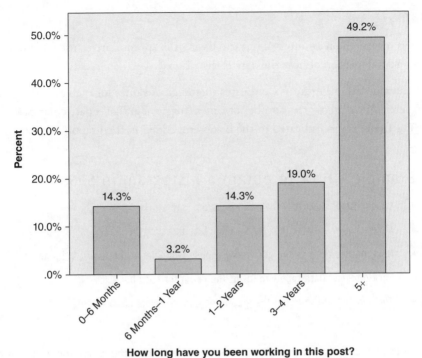

Figure 7.1 SPSS output: bar chart of time in post

Source: Campbell, 2015

Alternatively, a pie chart may be used to represent nominal data or ordinal data. The latter is data which comes from scaled questions where the responses represent degrees, for example, from strongly disagree to strongly agree, or numerically from 1–7 to represent a positive or negative attitude towards a specific question. The key issue to remember with both bar and pie charts is to keep the information simple and visually striking for the reader. Where too many categories are included, the images become confusing and difficult to read.

Points to note

The novice researcher is often enthusiastic when successfully generating a graph from SPSS, as it can be an onerous task for the beginner. However, always remember to think about the external viewer.

- Can they understand what you are trying to depict?
- Does the image convey the meaning that you wish?

Histograms

When data is measured on an interval or ratio basis, it is appropriate to use a histogram to facilitate a visual depiction of how the data is distributed.

The x axis (horizontal) in Figure 7.2 indicates the range of values for each of the cases whilst the y axis (vertical) will show the number of times (frequency) that a particular case is recorded. The frequency is indicated in the boxes embedded in the graph.

Example – How to obtain a histogram in SPSS

- Choose Graphs > Legacy Dialog > Histogram

- Move chosen variable into the variable box and click OK

- Next, double click on the graph and choose Elements at the top of the graph

- Click on Show Data Labels to insert the count for each bar

- Click on Edit at the top of the graph and choose Select Chart to add a graph frame.

The graph provided as SPSS output also shows the mean, standard deviation and number of respondents in the top right hand corner (see Figure 7.2).

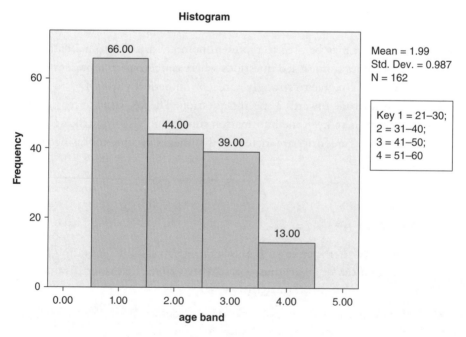

Figure 7.2 SPSS output: histogram of respondent cohort age band

Source: Campbell, 2015.

Scatter graphs

Scatter graphs are used when the researcher wishes to consider the relationship between two quantitative variables. In a social work survey of worker resilience, the research student wished to investigate the relationship between resilience and personal accomplishment. These aspects of the workers' attitude traits were measured by a psychometric test which produced numeric scores for each construct; resilience and personal accomplishment. In the scatter plot below, the y axis represents the values of one variable whilst the other variable is shown on the x axis and the points on the graph represent each sample unit. Scatter graphs can be used with interval, ratio or ordinal data.

Example – How to obtain a scatter graph in SPSS

- Choose Graphs > Legacy Dialog > Scatter/dot > Simple Scatter
- Click on Define > Move variables into y and x axes and click OK
- Click on Edit at the top of the graph and choose Select Chart to add a graph frame.

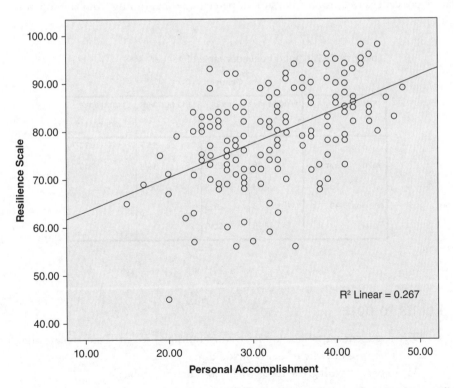

Figure 7.3 SPSS output: scatter plot showing linear relationship between resilience and personal accomplishment

Source: McFadden (2013) Resilience and burnout in child protection, PhD thesis, University of Ulster, p338.

Data represented through tables

A more detailed breakdown of the distribution of data can be obtained through frequency tables, which may be simple, relative and cumulative (all of which are generated via SPSS). The simple table (more commonly called 'frequency table') shows the numbers of value for each variable.

Example – How to obtain a frequency table in SPSS

- Choose Analyse › Descriptives › Frequencies

- Move selected variables from left hand box to right hand variable box and click OK.

The frequency table, depicted in Table 7.1 as an SPSS output, has a number of column headings, including value labels (male and female), frequency (or count of occurrence) per cent, valid per cent and cumulative per cent.

The valid per cent refers to the percentages with the omission of the missing values, whilst the cumulative per cent is the progressive sum of percentages beginning from the top of the table.

Table 7.1   SPSS output: frequency table of gender

Gender

		Frequency	per cent	valid per cent	cumulative per cent
	male	65	33.2	33.7	33.7
Valid	female	128	65.3	66.3	100.0
	Total	193	98.5	100.0	
Missing	99	3	1.5		
Total		196	100.0		

Points to note

- When presenting tables, information should be presented clearly and should be easy to process by the reader at first sight.
- Avoid overcrowding the table with too much information.
- Do not get zealous with over use of colours and/or patterns.

- Include a title that is relevant to the content of the table.
- Include a key where necessary to provide clarity.
- Maintain consistency when presenting table styles within a report and avoid a hotchpotch of table designs except where necessary to use different table formats according to data type.

Cross-tabulation tables are also available when using SPSS. These tables are a useful way of viewing data from two different variables to consider the difference across values within each of the variables compared. If two variables are measured at the categorical or ordinal levels, we assess their relationship by cross tabulating the data in a table.

A cross-tabulation table is a two-dimensional (rows x columns) table formed by 'cross-classifying' subjects or events on two categorical/ordinal variables. One variable's categories define the rows while the other variable's categories define the columns. The intersection (cross tabulation) of each row and column forms a cell, which displays the count (frequency) of cases classified as being in the applicable category of both variables. Below is a simple example of a hypothetical table that cross tabulates patient gender against survival of chest trauma:

	Survives	Dies	Total
Male	34	16	50
Female	7	43	50
Total	41	59	100

A study concerned with the mental health and well-being of young people (McColgan and Campbell, 2012) considered a number attendance patterns at a local youth club according to gender. When we look at the second row in Table 7.2 (% within gender) we see the comparison according to gender regarding attendance more than once a week, once weekly and fortnightly.

Example – How to obtain a cross-tabulation table in SPSS

- Choose Analyse > Descriptive statistics > Crosstabs
- Choose Variables and move into row and column boxes and click OK

→

- Click Cells box

- Click on Row, Column and Total Percentages box and observe counts box

- Click Continue

Table 7.2   SPSS output: cross-tabulation table of gender by patterns of attendance at a local youth club

			How often do you attend?			
			Once every two weeks	Once per week	More than once per week	Total
Gender	Male	Count	30	95	53	178
		% within Gender	16.8%	53.4%	29.8%	100.0%
		% within How often do you attend?	71.4%	48.5%	63.9%	55.5%
		% of Total	9.3%	29.6%	16.5%	55.5%
	Female	Count	12	101	30	143
		% within Gender	8.4%	70.6%	21.0%	100.0%
		% within How often do you attend?	28.5%	51.4%	36.2%	44.5%
		% of Total	3.7%	31.5%	9.3%	44.5%
Total		Count	42	196	83	321
		% within Gender	13.1%	61.1%	25.9%	100.0%
		% within How often do you attend?	100.0%	100.0%	100.0%	100.0%
		% of Total	13.1%	61.1%	25.8%	100.0%

Measures of central tendency and measures of dispersion

Graphs and tables are a high-impact method of considering the overall distribution of cases and a quick glance at a bar chart or histogram will indicate which value is approximately at the centre of the distribution. However, we may wish to consider this further and ask a question about the typical or mean value for a distribution.

Measures of central tendency include the mode, mean and median

The mode is the value in a distribution with the highest frequency (count). It can be used with all levels of measurement but is not appropriate in relation to interval data with

Table 7.3 SPSS output: current social work post

Years in practice	Frequency
1	3
2	6
3	4
4	6
5	2

many values. It is the only measure of central tendency that can be calculated for nominal (categorical) data and may be ascertained from the consideration of a frequency table. In Table 7.3, it is relatively easy to see the mode. However, what may occur, as in this example, is that there may be two categories which have the highest frequency and this is known as a bimodal distribution.

In addition, the median may be calculated with ordinal and interval/ratio data. If there is an odd number of cases, the median is the middle score and where there is an even number of cases, the median is the average of the two middle scores.

The mean can be used with interval/ratio data and is the sum of all scores in a distribution divided by the total number of scores.

Example – How to obtain mean, mode and median in SPSS

- Choose Analyse › Descriptive › Frequencies
- Move selected variables from left hand box to right hand variable box
- Click on 'statistics' and then click on 'Mean, Mode and Median' in the Central Tendency box
- Click on 'continue' and then click 'ok'.

The mean, median and mode of the age of 62 respondents in a survey of social worker attitudes to dual diagnosis are recorded in Table 7.4.

Table 7.4   SPSS output: mean, mode and median

Statistics

Age

Valid N		63
Missing		0
Mean		45.0952
Median		46.0000
Mode		40.00

Measures of dispersion

Measures of dispersion are descriptive statistics that tell us about the range and variability of scores within the data. One measure of dispersion is referred to as the 'range' which is obtained via a simple subtraction of the lowest score from the highest score in the cases.

For example:

- Group A have the following recorded scores for an essay submission: 54 55 58 63 65 68
- Group B have the following recorded scores: 57 58 59 60 62 65

The range of Group A is 68–54 = 14 and therefore the range is spread over fourteen units whilst the range of Group B is 65–57 = 8 and the range is spread over eight units. Therefore, Group A has a greater variability in scores than Group B.

In order to consider outliers in the data we use the interquartile range (IQR) which, as the name suggests, looks at the data in 'quarters'. It is calculated by placing the scores in ascending order, locating the upper value of the first quartile (the point below which 25 per cent of the scores lie) and subtracting it from the upper value of the third quartile (the point below which 75 per cent of the scores lie). Thus, the IQR is the distance between these two values. Whilst the IQR can indicate the spread it says nothing about the deviation from the mean scores.

This is calculated through the standard deviation and variance. The variance is the average of the distances of the individual scores from mean. The standard deviation is the square root of the variance (see Table 7.5).

Table 7.5   SPSS output: mean and standard deviation

Statistics

Age

	Valid N	63
	Missing	0
Mean		45.0952
Standard deviation		9.76451
Variance		95.346

Example – How to obtain standard deviation and variance in SPSS

- Choose Analyse > Descriptive > Frequencies
- Move selected variables from left hand box to right hand variable box
- Click on Statistics' and then click on Mean, Standard Deviation and Variance
- Click on Continue and then OK.

It is important to note that when you quote a mean it is good practice to provide the standard deviation. In addition, the sample size should also be included.

Which test?

The next stage of the data analysis process involves thinking about which test to use in accordance with data type and objectives of research. However, it is crucial to underline that this should have been determined at the beginning of the research process as the type of data collected determines to some extent the type of test to be used.

The following section will focus on the tests most commonly used by social work students in small-scale quantitative projects. It will utilise the procedures for obtaining tests and also for interpreting the results using the SPSS package. It will focus on:

- tests of association – chi-square and correlations;

- tests which look at difference between the means – t-tests (discussion on analysis of variance can be found in Sarantakos, 2010 and Pallant, 2013);

- non-parametric equivalents of Pearson's *r* correlations and t-tests.

See Table 7.6 for data consideration in the choice of tests.

Choosing the correct tests

Parametric tests are the most thorough and rigorous of statistical tests as they permit an in-depth statistical analysis of the data. However, parametric tests rely on data that is distributed in a certain way, i.e. normally, and it is recognised that a large number of data collected in social care research may not be normally distributed (otherwise known as a Gaussian distribution). The meaning of 'distributed' in this context refers to the frequency of occurrence of particular numbers. For example, a question in a survey could ask social workers how many new cases they have in a typical week and the responses could be around three to four. However, a number of respondents from different teams could respond on a range from two to ten. Parametric methods are utilised when we have knowledge that the population is approximately normal. It is possible to test that data distribution is normal using a variety of statistical tests (such as the Kolmogorov-Smirnov test), but this is beyond the scope of this chapter. Parametric methods are typically the first methods that we consider in the analysis of data; however, if in doubt about whether data are normally distributed it is safer to use non-parametric tests.

Non-parametric tests are used when data does not meet the criteria for a parametric test. Non-parametric tests do not rely on assumptions about the shape or parameters of the underlying population distribution. It is also appropriate to use non-parametric tests when the sample size is small or when the data collected is nominal or ordinal. They can, of course, be used with interval or ratio data when the data does not conform to a normal distribution.

Table 7.6 Popular bivariate parametric tests

Test name	Purpose	IV data consideration	DV data consideration
Pearson product moment correlation (*r*)	To ascertain the existence of a relationship (correlation) between two variables.	Interval or ratio	Interval, ratio
Independent sample t-test	To test the difference between the means of two independent groups, for example, men and women.	Nominal	Interval, ratio
Paired sample t-test	To test the difference between the means of a paired group.	Nominal	Interval, ratio
Analysis of variance (ANOVA)	To test the difference among means of three or more related groups, for example, marital status such as single, married, divorced.	Nominal	Interval, ratio

Table 7.7   Non-parametric statistical tests

Test name	Purpose	IV data consideration	DV data consideration
Chi-square test of independence	To test the predicted value of a proportion for a population.	Nominal	Nominal
Spearman rank order correlation (r)	To ascertain the existence of a relationship (correlation) between two variables.	Ordinal	Ordinal
Mann-Whitney U Test (U)	To test the difference in the ranks of scores of two independent groups.	Nominal	Ordinal
Wilcoxon signed ranks test (t or z)	To test the difference in the ranks of scores of two dependent groups.	Nominal	Ordinal

The tables above depict a number of tests that are commonly used in small-scale research projects. The list is divided into parametric and non-parametric tests and are labelled according to purpose, data considerations, and whether the variables are independent (IV) or dependent (DV).

The following sections discuss some of the tests referred to in Table 7.7, providing information on how to conduct the tests via SPSS and a concomitant discussion of the outputs.

Tests for association

Cross-tabulations tables are explained on page 105 and are used to look at the descriptive relationship between two or more variables. The chi-square test is utilised to look at the significance of the relationship between variables and is often used in conjunction with the cross tabulations. The chi-square test may be used with nominal (categorical or ranked) data.

Chi-square tests

Example – Chi-square test

The example is taken from a study of the mental health and well-being of young people in a region of Northern Ireland (McColgan and Campbell, 2012). The cross-tabulation table (Table 7.8) and the subsequent chi-square statistic (Table 7.9) considered the response to a simple yes/no question on attendance at a youth club according to gender. From Table 7.8 it is clear that a higher percentage of female respondents attend the youth club.

Table 7.8 SPSS output: cross-tabulation table of gender by yes/no response regarding attendance at a local youth club

			Do you attend a youth club?		
			Yes	No	Total
Gender	Male	Count	181	177	358
		% within Gender	**50.6%**	49.4%	100.0%
		% within Do you attend a youth club?	56.0%	67.3%	61.1%
		% of Total	30.9%	30.2%	61.1%
	Female	Count	142	86	228
		% within Gender	**62.3%**	37.7%	100.0%
		% within Do you attend a youth club?	44.0%	32.7%	38.9%
		% of Total	24.2%	14.7%	38.9%
Total		Count	323	263	586
		% within Gender	55.1%	44.9%	100.0%
		% within Do you attend a youth club?	100.0%	100.0%	100.0%
		% of Total	55.1%	44.9%	100.0%

The most important facet of the SPSS chi-square test output (Table 7.9) is the Pearson chi-square. The value is shown at 7.73 with one degree of freedom (df) and with a two-tailed significance level of $p = .005$. The result is usually reported as $\chi 2\ (1) = 7.73, p < .01$. This means that there is a significant association between the two variables and if we consult the cross tabulation above it is clear that a higher percentage of females attend the local youth centre.

Correlations

Correlations (and primarily Pearson's r correlations) are used by researchers to ascertain the existence of a relationship between two variables. The data used in the statistical procedure is interval or ratio (Scott and Mazhindu, 2005). If the sample size is below thirty then the non-parametric equivalent for ranked data, the Spearman rho statistical test, should be used. In addition, the Spearman rho test should also be used when the data is ranked or taken from a Likert scale (a question which has answers on a scaled basis, e.g. strongly disagree, disagree, unsure, agree, strongly agree).

Table 7.9 SPSS output: chi-square table of gender by yes/no response regarding attendance at a local youth club

	Value	df	Asymp. Sig. (2-sided)	Fisher Exact Sig. (2-sided)	Fisher Exact Sig. (1-sided)
Pearson chi-square	7.737[a]	1	.005		
Continuity correction[b]	7.270	1	.007		
Likelihood ratio	7.787	1	.005		
Fisher's exact test				.006	.003
Linear-by-linear association	7.724	1	.005		
Number of valid cases	586				

a. 0 cells (0.0%) have expected count less than 5. The minimum expected count is 102.33.

b. Computed only for a 2x2 table.

A correlation can either be positive or negative. In a positive correlation, as the values of one variable increases so does the other; for example, as a worker's years in practice increase his salary may also increase. In a negative correlation there is usually an inverse relationship between both variables, i.e. where the value of one variable decreases the other increases; for example, an increase in exercise and a decrease in emotional well-being problems.

Points to note

- Measurement must be interval or ratio scale.
- Samples must be random and have normal distribution.
- Do plot your data prior to performing the correlation (see page 103 for scatter plots).
- The relationship between the variables is associative only and this does not infer causation.
- Use Spearman rho when data is ranked or the sample is small.

Example – Correlation

A Pearson's r correlation was performed on data gathered from 53 undergraduate social work students on the first year of a degree programme. It considered whether there was a relationship between marks obtained in psychology and preparation for practice (PFP) modules. The following steps were taken in the calculation of the correlation via SPSS.

→

Calculate a correlation with SPSS:

- Choose Analyse > Correlate > Bivariate
- Select Variables and move to the variables box
- Click on Pearson
- Click OK

Looking at the output in Table 7.10 it is apparent that the result is significant at the 0.01 level, i.e. the Sig. 2 tailed row in the box shows a p value of $< .01$ which is a highly significant result.

It is also very important to look at the r value and in this case it is .382 which means that it is a medium strength correlation. (It is widely accepted that a correlation of $r = .10$ represents a small effect size, $r = .30$ indicates a medium effect size and $r = .5$ and above represents a large effect size (Cohen, 1992).

Table 7.10   SPSS output from the Pearson r correlation calculation

		psychology	PFP
psychology	Pearson correlation	1	.382**
	Sig. (2-tailed)		.005
	N	53	53
PFP	Pearson correlation	.382**	1
	Sig. (2-tailed)	.005	
	N	53	53

** Correlation is significant at the 0.01 level (2-tailed).

The results should be reported as r (53) = .382, p < .01. This means that there is a significant and fairly strong positive correlation between social work student marks on the psychology and preparation for practice (PFP) modules.

Spearman rho: a non-parametric test equivalent to the Pearson r correlation

As stated above, when the sample size is small or there is ranked data, a non-parametric equivalent for ranked data, the Spearman rho statistical test, should be employed.

Example – Spearman rho

In a study of addictions workers (social worker and nurse trained) and their attitudes toward issues of dual diagnosis, a number of Spearman rho correlations were used to examine the relationship between the variable 'worker understanding of dual diagnosis issues' and those which considered respondent knowledge and confidence in working with drug issues, harm reduction and relapse prevention.

Calculate a Spearman rho with SPSS:

- Choose Analyse › Correlate› Bivariate

- Click on Spearman

- Select Variables and move to the variables box

- Click OK.

On consideration of the output table below (see Table 7.11), there are strong positive and significant correlations between 'understanding of dual diagnosis issues' and each of the following variables:

1. confidence when working with drug issues (Rs = .350 p = .00);

2. harm reduction (Rs = .663 p = .00);

3. knowledge of relapse prevention (Rs = .451 p = .00).

All the reported correlations are statistically significant, i.e. all are less than the critical value of .05 and indeed are seen as highly significant as they are less than .01 (see page 98 for further explanation on p values).

This suggests that a greater knowledge of drug-related issues is positively related to a greater understanding of dual diagnosis issues for this respondent group (see Table 7.11).

Tests of mean scores

Independent and paired samples t-tests

The following two tests are often used to establish the significance in difference between the means of two scores. The independent samples t-test is used to test for a difference in the means of two samples of unrelated scores.

Table 7.11 SPSS output from Spearman rho correlations between respondents' understanding of dual diagnosis issues and drug issues

		How would you describe your understanding of dual diagnosis issues?	I am confident in working with people with a range of drug use issues	How would you rate your knowledge of Harm Reduction?	How would you rate your knowledge of Relapse Prevention?
How would you describe your understanding of dual diagnosis issues?	Correlation Coefficient	1.000	.350**	.663**	.451**
	Sig. (2-tailed)	.	.005	.000	.000
	N	63	63	61	59

Example – Independent *t*-test

An independent *t*-test was performed on the same data gathered from 53 undergraduate social work students on the first year of a degree programme to consider the difference in mean scores on an exam for female and male students.

Calculate an independent t-test with SPSS:

- Choose Analyse› Compare Means › Independent Samples t-test
- Select Variable and move to the Test Variable Box (in this example the test variable is Psychology Exam Marks)
- Click on Grouping Variable and move gender into Dialog Box
- Click on Define Groups
- Place value 1 (male) in group 1 box and value (female) in group 2 box
- Click continue and OK.

Table 7.12 shows some descriptive statistics for the variable labelled psychology: N = the number of marks recorded for the psychology exam according to male and female groupings. The table also shows the mean score for each group, standard deviation and standard error of the mean.

Table 7.12 SPSS output 1 from independent *t*-test calculation

	Gender	N	Mean	Standard deviation	Standard error mean
psychology	male	16	58.6250	11.86522	2.96630
	female	37	62.1892	9.47757	1.55810

Table 7.13 indicates the *t*-test result. Firstly, we consider the Levene's test for equality of variances to help you decide whether the assumption of equal variance is met. The result from this test is non-significant ($F = 2.543, p = .117$) which tells us that the variances of the two groups are not significantly different and equal variances are assumed. As a result, we do not read the results on the second line which are only used when there are significant differences in variances of the two groups. Therefore, on reading across the top line of numbers, we can see that there are no significant differences in the mean scores of the two groups. The results of the analysis are written as follows:

An independent samples *t*-test showed that male student marks ($M = 58.6, SD = 11.86$) were not significantly lower than female student marks ($M = 62.1, SD = 9.47$), $t(51) = -1.16, p > .05$.

The mean scores are not significantly different and this cannot be attributed to chance as the *p* value is greater than the critical value of .05 (see page 98 for further explanation on *p* values).

Table 7.13 SPSS output 2 from independent *t*-test calculation

Independent Samples Test

	Levene's Test for Equality of Variances		t-test for Equality of Means					95% Confidence Interval of the Difference	
	F	Sig.	t	df	Sig. (2-tailed)	Mean Difference	Std. Error Difference	Lower	Upper
psychology Equal variances assumed	2.543	.117	-1.164	51	.250	-3.56419	3.06325	-9.71393	2.58555
Equal variances not assumed			-1.064	23.668	.298	-3.56419	3.35062	-10.48466	3.35628

Paired samples *t*-test

The paired sample *t*-test is a repeated measures test to consider the impact of treatment before and after a specific intervention. This is called a repeated measures design as we are repeating the measures on the same group of participants.

Example – Paired samples *t*-test

A project that looked at the impact of a range of community group interventions to address mental health and emotional well-being in Northern Ireland used the Rosenberg self-esteem test to evaluate the impact of a group intervention on the self-esteem of the participants. The Rosenberg self-esteem scale (RSES), developed by sociologist Dr Morris Rosenberg, is a self-esteem measure widely used in social-science research. The RSES is designed similar to social-survey questionnaires. It is a ten-item Likert scale, with items answered on a four-point scale – from strongly agree to strongly disagree. The scale measures self-esteem by asking the respondents to reflect on their current feelings. Scores may range from 0 to 30; scores between 15 and 25 are considered within normal range and scores below 15 suggest low self-esteem.

$\longrightarrow$

Calculate a paired samples *t*-test with SPSS:

- Choose Analyse› Compare Means › Paired-Samples *t*-test

- Move the selected variable to the test variable 1 box (in this example the test variable 1 is pre-score) and do the same for test variable 2 box (in this example the test variable 2 is post-score)

- Click on Grouping Variable and move gender into Dialog Box

- Click on Define Groups

- Place value 1 (male) in group 1 box and value (female) in group 2 box

- Click Continue and OK.

Table 7.14 shows some descriptive statistics for the variables labelled pre-score and post-score, N = the number of scores for time one and two, the mean score for each group, standard deviation and standard error of the mean.

A paired sample *t*-test was conducted to analyse the difference in Rosenberg group scores for (n = 54) participants in a programme which considered mental health awareness for men at the pre- and post-intervention stages. The results of the analysis from Table 7.14 may be documented as follows: There was a significant difference in the scores for time one ($M = 18.2$, $SD = 4.1$) and time two ($M = 21.6$ $SD = 4.1$) conditions; $t (54) = -7.86, p = . 000$).

The *p* value in the equation shows a highly significant difference between the two scores as it is calculated as less than the critical value of 0.05. The initial group score was recorded in the normal self-esteem banding (18.2) but results did show a further significant rise in self-esteem as a result of the programme (21.6).

Table 7.14 SPSS output from paired-samples *t*-test calculation

Paired Samples Test

		Paired Differences							
				Std. Error	95% Confidence Interval of the Difference				
		Mean	Std. Deviation	Mean	Lower	Upper	t	df	Sig. (2-tailed)
Pair 1	Pre Score - Post Score	-3.43636	3.24188	.43713	-4.31277	-2.55996	-7.861	54	.000

Non-parametric paired samples – Wilcoxon signed-rank test

If we wished to look at group differences for ordinal data at pre- and post-intervention junctures, we would use the non-parametric equivalent test called the Wilcoxon signed-rank test. The procedure tests the null hypothesis that the population distributions for the two sets of scores are the same against the alternative hypothesis that they are not the same.

Example – Paired samples Wilcoxon signed-rank test

The following example draws upon an analysis of ranked (ordinal data) that was gathered in respect of student knowledge acquisition as a result of a postgraduate module on methods of social work assessment. Fourteen postgraduate students completed the questionnaire and as the numbers were small and the data was ordinal it was decided to use a non-parametric test to consider any differences in knowledge attained at the pre- and post-teaching stages.

Calculate a paired samples Wilcoxon signed-rank test with SPSS:

*   Choose Analyse> Non-Parametric tests > Legacy dialog box > 2 related samples

*   Move two selected variables into variables 1 and 2 boxes

*   Tick Wilcoxon box

*   Click Continue and OK.

Table 7.15 shows the number of negative ranks (the number of times the rank of variable 1 is less than the rank of variable 2) and the positive ranks (the number of times the rank of variable 1 is greater than the rank of variable 2). The notes below Table 7.15 show the direction of the differences in rank scores; in this case there was a greater number of positive ranks, i.e. the rating of knowledge after teaching on assessment models was higher after the module.

The results from Table 7.16 should be reported as follows: A Wilcoxon signed-rank test showed that the knowledge of the thirteen students was significantly higher after the programme $Z = -3.176, p = .01$.

Table 7.15   SPSS output 1 from Wilcoxon signed-rank test calculation

		N	Mean rank	Sum of ranks
Rate knowledge of assessment	Negative Ranks	0[a]	.00	.00
models (After) - Rate knowledge	**Positive Ranks**	12[b]	6.50	78.00
of assessment models (Before)	Ties	1[c]		
	Total	13		

a. Rate knowledge of assessment models (After) < Rate knowledge of assessment models (Before)

b. Rate knowledge of assessment models (After) > Rate knowledge of assessment models (Before)

c. Rate knowledge of assessment models (After) = Rate knowledge of assessment models (Before)

Table 7.16   SPSS output 2 from Wicoxon signed-rank test calculation

Test statistics[a]

	Rate knowledge of assessment models (After) - Rate knowledge of assessment models (Before)
Z	-3.176[b]
Asymp. Sig. (2-tailed)	**.001**

a. Wilcoxon signed-ranks test

b. Based on negative ranks

Summary

This chapter has focused on:

- summarising the basic statistical procedures used in small-scale research projects;
- providing a synopsis of how to conduct a number of procedures in SPSS, including the creation of graphs, tables and descriptive statistics;
- a brief overview of how to utilise and interpret inferential statistics, for example, correlations and *t*-test procedures and showed how to report them within the content of a research report;
- offering indicators to further reading to help you to learn more about the use of advanced techniques in statistical analysis.

Further reading

Argyrous, G (2006) *Statistics for Research, with a guide to SPSS*. London: SAGE.

Cronk, B (2016) *How to use SPSS: A step by step guide to analysis and interpretation* (9th edition). Glendale, CA: Pyrczak Publishing.

Pallant, J (2013) *SPSS Survival Manual: A step by step guide to data analysis using SPSS*. Maidenhead: Open University Press.

Sirkin, M (2006) *Statistics for the Social Sciences*. London: SAGE.

8: Presenting Results and Findings

Chapter aims

This chapter will:

- offer guidance on how to present research, audit and service evaluation projects;
- focus particularly on the presentation of results and findings, but will also briefly cover other aspects of presentation such as structure, writing an abstract and limitations of the study;
- consider the essential elements and types of presentation, including both oral and written, and the need to relate the message to the audience;
- help you to choose the correct method of presentation to make your findings effective;
- offer guidance on presenting quantitative, qualitative and mixed-methods studies;
- explore methods of presentation using tables, bar charts and graphs;
- illustrate key aspects using examples from social work projects;
- offer some general points about presentation in written documents.

Introduction: the audience and the message

It is conventional to refer to *results* of quantitative studies and *findings* of qualitative studies. In this chapter we use both terms where we are referring to both quantitative and quantitative studies, except where this becomes too cumbersome.

Perhaps the first question to ask in relation to presenting the results or findings of your research, audit or service evaluation project concerns exactly why you are presenting. Is it a requirement of the research funding body? Do you feel a professional duty to disseminate so as to build up the knowledge base of the profession? Do you want to raise questions, provoke new thoughts or improve policy and practice? Is it a course requirement or for your own career development? Being clear on these sorts of questions is essential to deciding on what you will present and how.

The selection of the most appropriate mode of presentation flows from your purpose. For example, you might be considering a written report, a journal article, a book chapter or a news item. You might be considering an oral presentation within your organisation. Or you may be presenting at a conference or delivering a conference poster, a one-page summary distributed by email within an organisation, or a web page as part of the website of the organisation or university department where the project was conducted. Ask yourself what is the most appropriate mode for your purpose? You might, of course, use more than one mode of presentation.

The essential dynamic is to connect the potential audience with the material that you propose to present to them and use that to decide on the mode of presentation and the detail of what to include. Who is your target audience? Why might people be interested in what you want to present? What is new and informative that you have to offer readers or those attending? If you are intending to write an article for a magazine or journal, what sort of people – such as what range of professions or countries – read that journal? Before you start writing or preparing your slideshow for a talk, consider the audience and the interests, knowledge and questions that they will have. If you are presenting in written or web form, do not forget that the publication may go to people beyond those that you initially envisage. How will respondents, professionals, managers, policy makers, the general public or the media engage with your material?

For a journal article or book chapter you will need to consider particularly what you want to say that is original, and who might be interested to hear what you have to say. You will need to consider how much will you say in this particular article. For example, an academic audience may appreciate an increased emphasis on theoretical material that would not be appreciated by practitioners in the field. You should also bear in mind that a journal article will be regarded as a record of work done for future reference and secondary research. The literature review that you undertake may become a reference point for others interested in the topic. Honesty is required but you should not feel under pressure to present all the findings in one paper if they are more appropriately structured into two articles, perhaps for different audiences. Consider what is most important for your audience.

Main elements of your presentation

The basic structure of any presentation of research, professional audit or service evaluation will be:

- context;

- method;

- results or findings; and

- discussion.

At the start of the presentation you will need to include a title, author details and acknowledgements. This may seem obvious but experience has taught us not to assume that people know this, even among experienced social workers! You will also need to write an abstract or summary of the project.

The title should be clear, concise and precise. Every word counts! You may wish to try to make it attention-grabbing, but it is important not to be gimmicky. Eliminate all redundant words. It is not necessary to include terms such as 'an exploration of'; if the study includes a qualitative dimension, this will be apparent from the use of such terms as 'experiences of' or 'perspectives of'. You might ask yourself how the title would appear to a fellow health and social care professional or in an electronic search of a database or the internet. Depending on the type of publication or oral presentation, you might also like to consider how the title will appear to an international audience. Issues arise if you are referring to statutes or policy documents, or using terms that are particular to your country such as 'looked after children', or 'deprivation of liberty standards'. Some examples of titles of research, professional audit and service evaluation projects are given below.

Example – Titles of research, audit and service evaluation projects

- Decision making by vulnerable adult practitioners.

- Social work perspectives on the use of sponsored day care as a form of family support.

- Foster carer and social worker perspectives of foster placement disruption.

- Perceptions of child protection managers on the Health and Social Care Trust's *Guidance on Case Management of Allegations of Sexual Abuse where Alleged Adult Offenders have Contact with Children*.

- Dying fifteen years early: Traveller men's perceptions of what they and relevant agencies can do.

- You talkin' to me? Direct observations – a complex process made easier by effective communication.

- Assessing child neglect – an evaluation of the use of the graded care profile (GCP) for the assessment of child neglect by social work staff.

→

- Do newly qualified social workers feel ready for practice in child protection settings and are they willing to stay?

- Incidence of suicidal ideation and behaviour among young people known to the 16+ plus teams between April 2013 and April 2014.

- Mental health workers' perceptions of role, self-efficacy and organisational climate regarding the ethos of recovery.

- Trauma and homelessness: the experiences of homeless people in a city centre hostel.

(with acknowledgement to various students on the MSc Professional Development in Social Work at the University of Ulster, Northern Ireland)

Together with your name and those of any other authors, you should include the appropriate ascription to indicate the role in which you undertook the project. It is customary in journal articles and conference presentations and posters for students to include as a co-author their tutor who has spent time and energy supervising the project; in fact, any key person from your university/organisation involved in the detail of the project could be included as a co-author.

Some *acknowledgements* will need to be included near the start or end of the presentation. This may be acknowledging participants in the study and those professionals and managers who enabled you to access your data. If you are on a course of study you should acknowledge your tutor or supervisor unless he or she is a co-author. You will be ethically (and possibly legally) obliged to acknowledge any source of funding for the project, or if the project is undertaken as part of a course of study. In a written presentation you may end the acknowledgements with some variation on the traditional 'views expressed are those of the authors…'.

You need to consider the ethical and legal aspects of presenting your study. Who owns the intellectual property rights? If you are undertaking the project as part of a course of study you will need to check this with your tutor and the university. If the project is undertaken in your role as an employee, then the organisation probably owns the intellectual property rights. An employer may veto or delay publication if the material might seriously detract from the organisation's public credibility. This is an important part of their responsibility whether they are a public body or a charity dependent on public support. For example, the topic may be too sensitive at this time, until action is taken to redress issues raised by the study. Work carried out in your role as employee will require consent from your employer to be published outside the organisation. You will need to ensure anonymity of data about individuals in accordance with ethical approval requirements, whether research, audit or service evaluation. In some situations, such as studies that cross teams, departments or organisations, you may wish to provide anonymity to these organisations and organisational units.

If you are presenting your results or findings as a journal article you will need to write an *abstract* summarising the article within a given number of words, usually between 150 and 250.

For some organisational reports you may also have to write a summary of a specified length. The abstract or summary should be structured in the same way as the whole article or report and should include context, methods, results (findings) and discussion. Note that the abstract is not an introduction, it is not a contents list and it is not like a film trailer designed to whet the appetite without giving away the plot! The abstract must include brief, accurate details of the method and the main result or finding, as well as some indication of the implications of the study in a sentence (or two). The abstract should contain no references. An example follows.

Example – Abstract

Day support services are a neglected aspect of promoting the health and social well-being of vulnerable adults within the community. Recent policy developments highlight the need to make services more needs-centred and to promote social inclusion. Perceptions of day support provision were explored using quantitative and qualitative questionnaires with clients (54), family carers (7) and a range of health and social services staff (36) and other organisations (10) regarding day support services provided by one Health and Social Services Trust in Northern Ireland. These questionnaires were followed by focus groups to explore key themes. A theoretical framework to shape the evaluation was derived from the work of Maslow and Wolfensberger. A diverse and complex range of health and social care needs were met through day support provision. The engagement of service users seemed patchy in terms of both information provision and consultation. Publicly funded transport was widely regarded as key to accessibility of services. Younger clients did not find current provision attractive, and desired more flexible opening hours. The development of skills for, and support for transition to, employment seemed underdeveloped. For family carers, day support services provided respite that was much valued although clients were not always aware of their family carer's needs. Day support services have an important role within community care, but this is little recognised. Day support services need to be appraised within the context of meeting more complex health and social care needs in the community and emerging policy directions such as the management of risk and the desirability and cost-effectiveness of support for family carers.

(Fleming and Taylor, 2010 pp66–76).

The context section of your report or oral presentation might be considered in three parts: (1) why the topic is important and the context (introduction); (2) the theoretical framework that you are using to conceptualise the study and (3) why this has been selected (theory chapter); and what is already known on this topic in terms of empirical research (literature review).

The introductory material on why the topic is important will vary considerably according to the audience, but should essentially enable the reader to get his or her bearings in terms of the prevalence or incidence of this problem or the development of this area of service provision, usually including law, policy, regulations, standards, organisational arrangements and practice issues. Key terms should be defined in this chapter, referring the reader to a glossary as necessary. The historical context of developing services should be briefly outlined as appropriate. This section may usefully be structured from the big picture narrowing down to the particular issue that has prompted your study. The context needs to be suitably comprehensive but readable, and justify the study topic or question. It should clarify the question to be addressed or explored. It might be viewed like a detective novel with an exciting plot! The research question is the tension (murder!) at the start which will be unravelled and solved. Below is an example of summarising theoretical material. Chapter 1 gives detailed guidance on summarising what is already known from empirical research on a particular topic.

Example – A theoretical context for a study

In more recent work Brodzinsky (2006) defined two types of openness in modern adoption. The first is 'communicative openness', i.e. openness in sharing of information with the child about his or her background and origins. The second is 'structural openness', i.e. placements where there are built-in arrangements for ongoing post adoption contact between adopters, adopted children and birth family members. This move towards greater openness has brought challenges for adoptive parents (Ryburn, 1998). In parallel with this, the way in which agencies recruit, train and assess prospective adopters has developed to assist prospective adopters in their under-standing of an adopted child's need to adjust to their adopted status and in knowing the role that they, as adoptive parents, play in this psychological adjustment. It is now a prerequisite of being approved as prospective adopters that applicants can appreciate that it is beneficial for a child to learn from their adoptive parents about their adoptive status and background appropri-ate to their stage of development as they mature from childhood toward adulthood and some form of contact is now common practice in the United Kingdom (Neill, 2004: McSherry et al., 2008). Prospective adopters are generally accepting of the fact that their adopted child will have indirect contact with their child's birth family in the form of an exchange of letters and pho-tographs. In some instances adoptive parents agree to face-to-face contact between siblings, perhaps where siblings are adopted by different carers. However, practice experience suggests that they tend to have more reservations about taking this appreciation of the child's birth family a step further to consider the challenges of post adoption face-to-face contact with birth parents.

(Turkington and Taylor, 2009, pp21–38).

The methods section of your report or oral presentation needs to explain clearly how you went about studying this question. The main components are likely to be:

- the overall design or approach to the study;
- sampling;
- data collection tool(s);

- ethical approval and access to data; and

- method of analysis.

The amount of detail on method will depend on the type of presentation. A presentation for busy managers and professionals involved in this service area is likely to include only a minimum on methods, and will focus instead on the results or findings. A report or journal article would need to contain fuller details of the method so that someone else could replicate the study to verify the results or would need to undertake a comparison using the same method with another sample in another organisation or country.

The first part of the section on results or findings should describe the actual data sample or respondents. The methods section will have included the proposed data gathering, for example, the distribution of the survey or the proposed group to be invited to participate in qualitative interviews. The results section of a survey will report at the start how many responded in relation to the number invited to do so and other basic socio-demographic data. The findings section in a qualitative study will begin with a brief profile of those who participated in the interviews or focus groups, in terms of relevant characteristics (see Table 8.1).

The results or findings presented need to be a focused and coherent set, in a logical sequence. The presentation must make sense to the reader or listener, and gradually develop their understanding as the presentation progresses. The sequence of presentation of results or findings does not have to follow the sequence of the questionnaire or interview questions, although it commonly does so. There should be a logical flow, unfolding the building blocks and linkages in developing the results or findings. We discuss below particular issues in presenting qualitative, quantitative and mixed-methods studies, including visual presentation of data.

Table 8.1 Characteristics of participants by location, gender and experience

	Location				Gender		Years in this work	
Staff group	1	2	3	4	M	F	Min*	Max
CG	1	1	1	1	2	2	11	17
GP	1	1	1	1	4	0	10	25
SW	5	7	4	2	7	11	1	14
Other CM	1	1	4	5	1	10	1	15
Comm N	5	8	2	4	1	18	1	25
OT	5	3	4	8	0	20	3	24
HC	0	6	3	2	1	10	1	18

(Continued)

Table 8.1 (Continued)

	Location				Gender		Years in this work	
Staff group	1	2	3	4	M	F	Min*	Max
Hosp Disch	3	4	4	1	1	11	1.5	13
Total	21	31	23	24	17	82		
	Total = 99				Total = 99			

Key to participants in the study

*Omitting students. 1/2/3/4 = Location by Health and Social Service Trust.

CG = consultant geriatrician.

GP = general medical practitioner.

SW = social work.

Other CM = other care managers (i.e. professions other than social work).

Comm N = community nursing.

OT = occupational therapy.

HC = managers of home care staff.

Hosp Disch = hospital discharge team (includes hospital social workers).

(from Taylor and Donnelly, 2006b, pp239–256)

Presentation of qualitative information

In a qualitative study the findings themselves will create the order of presentation. Typically, the strongest or most important themes are presented first. The structure of the study findings may themselves be the structure used for presentation, as illustrated in the example below. You generally explain the theme in your own words, illustrating the theme at intervals with edited quotations from the interviews or focus group sessions. The theme may be expanded with aspects of the theme (nuances, contradictions) also illustrated with quotes if possible. This is then repeated with other themes.

Example – Structuring qualitative results

Respondents recognised the categories of abuse used in documents by professionals in terms of physical, financial, verbal, psychological (emotional) abuse and neglect. In no focus group was sexual abuse mentioned until raised by the researcher. Two broad categories relating to older people's understanding of elder abuse emerged from the data. The first category of understanding of abuse of older people related to broader 'societal abuse' encompassing notions of respect and the qualities that confer distinct individuality, including attributes such as agency to act, self-awareness and having a past and a future. Secondly, the concept of the abuse of older people was understood at the level of the individual which was seen to affect a minority of older people. Key issues in this latter category were (1) the emotional underpinning of most or all abuse; (2) the vulnerability of the older person; (3) the intention of the (alleged) perpetrator; and (4) concepts of family duties and relationships. These concepts are explored in turn below.

(Taylor et al., 2014)

It is common to illustrate a poignant point with just one quote, and you should not use a quote more than once. Be clear what each quote illustrates or represents, and select the length of quotes to make them understandable. It is not necessary to include large sections from interviews. To do so can be tedious for the reader.

Ensure that the quote is understandable and separate from the original transcript that gave it context. If necessary, add an explanatory word in square brackets []. You should add an indicator of the source to all quotes to indicate the breadth of respondents you have cited, and to ensure that you are not over-quoting one individual. You should avoid giving a quote that virtually repeats the sentence you have just written in your own words. Quotes that are one sentence or less are run on within the paragraph as illustrated in the example below. Quotes that are more than one sentence are presented indented on a new line.

Example – Theme illustrated by a quote within the paragraph

Fear of burglary and assault featured surprisingly often in responses, across all Trusts, as a specific fear of many older people. Older people were perceived as being particularly vulnerable. 'We've had a lot of burglaries involving older people who've been robbed for maybe [only] £10 or £20 but it leaves very high psychological effects.' (Care Manager, Trust 1). Sometimes fear of burglary or assault was linked explicitly to the desire of the older person to enter admission to institutional care, and feelings of vulnerability even led some older people to refuse services.

(Taylor and Donnelly, 2006a, pp807-26)

The findings need to be integrated with what is already known on the topic (as in your literature review) so as to build on our generalisable understanding. However, the presentation must be clear as to which findings are from your study, and what material is from the literature. A key issue in presentation of qualitative studies is how to integrate with existing knowledge yet also maintain this distinction. In a small-scale study it is generally most straightforward and acceptable to present your findings in a findings section, and then to integrate with previous literature and theory in a following discussion section. For a larger study, the findings might be grouped into major sections, with the linking to appropriate literature following each one.

Presentation of quantitative data

Quantitative data lends itself to visual presentation. Charts and graphs can convey more detailed information clearly and efficiently where appropriate. Charts and graphs make the report more interesting and grab the reader's attention, although our advice is to use visual or graphical representation judiciously. You are trying to present the data in a manner that allows the reader to grasp quickly what the data means. It is the job of the title and wording on the visual to tell the reader what particular numbers mean.

Table 8.2   A graph presenting quantitative data in respect of autism by year of referral

Members in day centre by age bands of the various groupings						
Day centre members	In day centre		Received specialist visual assessment		Research group	
Age band	No	%	No	%	No	%
20–29	20	19.8	9	14.8	4	19.0
30–39	34	33.7	23	37.7	5	23.8
40–49	30	29.7	19	31.1	8	38.1
50–59	14	13.9	9	14.8	4	19.0
60+	3	3.0	1	1.6	0	–
Total	101	–	61		21	–
Mean age in years	38.5		38.8		39.7	

Source: Morrison, 2008, p56; findings published as Morrison et al., 2010, pp168–74

A *table* is a display of data that otherwise would be presented in text. If you need to show correspondence between one set of numbers and another, use a table. This can be particularly appropriate where you are demonstrating a simple correspondence between variables (bivariate relationship – called 'cross tab' in SPSS). See Table 8.2.

A bar chart or histogram shows the frequency of occurrence of a variable, and emphasises highest and lowest categories to show the distribution. Frequencies are on the vertical axis; categories on the horizontal axis. Data values are grouped into categories if necessary. See Figure 8.1.

If there is a trend or an interesting picture emerging use a graph. A line graph shows the trend for one variable over time, as in the example in Figure 8.2. A multiple line graph could be used to compare the trends for two or more variables over time.

All tables and graphs should be sufficiently complete with their labelling that they could stand on their own. As well as a clear title, it is important that each axis or column is labelled so as to define the data. The scales for the x and y axis in a graph or bar chart must be clear. Convey one message per figure or chart, and make that message the heading. Usually start a numerical axis at zero ('0'), or make it very clear if not. Make sure all scaling is similar to void distortion. Note that changing scaling can influence how people see the importance of the data (Taylor, 2013), as illustrated in Figure 8.3. Note that by convention tables are labelled at the top, figures at the bottom.

All tables, charts and graphs must be referenced from the text. You should summarise tables and graphs in the main text, not repeat all of the same material. The main text must be complete in itself, including summarising key points from graphs, charts and tables, with the

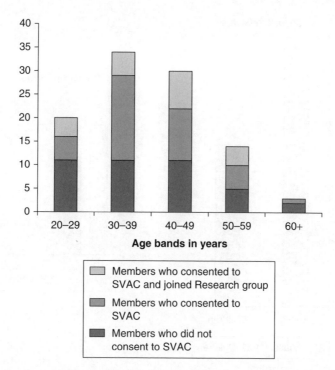

Figure 8.1 Illustration of a stacked bar chart presenting quantitative data. Number by band of the three main groups of individuals within the Resource Centre (SVAC refers to a Specialist Visual Assessment Clinic)

Source: McGlade, 2007.

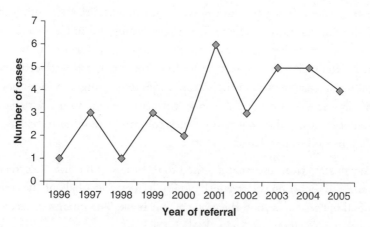

Figure 8.2 Illustration of a graph presenting quantitative data in respect of autism by year of referral. (From a report for a study published as Morrison et al., 2010, pp168–74)

visuals providing additional information that is not absolutely essential to the main argument. Visual materials must be accurate, and designed to be informative and reproduce well whether on a slide for an oral presentation or when printed in black and white.

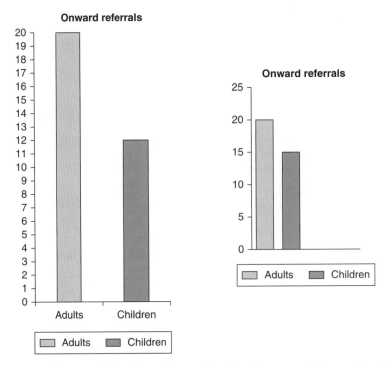

Figure 8.3 Illustration of impact of changing scales on a bar chart in respect of the number of adult and children referrals made to external agencies. (From report for study published as Morrison et al., 2010, pp168–74)

Use of pie charts is generally not recommended. As documents are rarely produced in colour, each sector needs to be carefully labelled if it is to be meaningful in black and white. It is not easy to compare sector sizes visually, so numbers for each sector need to be included. Also they are expensive to print. 3D pie charts suffer from these issues as well as the issue of being visually misleading in that the size of the sectors varies depending on where they appear around the diagram, so the visual size does not represent the data value. Bar charts allow for easy comparison of values, and do not require each column (data item) to be labelled, so are a preferable visual method to pie charts.

There is an array of statistical tests that are used to test the significance of correlations between variables as well as to report on the strength of correlations. Detail about the standard presentation of all of these is beyond the scope of this book. The interested reader is referred to the clear and authoritative book by Jackie Pallant (2013).

Presentation of mixed-methods studies

For a mixed-methods study that gathers both quantitative and qualitative data, it is common to present the quantitative data on a topic and then illustrate this with qualitative data.

This pattern is then repeated with the next topic and the results. The quantitative results present the measure of prevalence or incidence, which is then illustrated with qualitative findings. This sequence is illustrated in the example below.

Example – A sequence of quantitative followed by qualitative data on a topic in a mixed-methods study

Many (n=36, 80%) respondents did not think that they needed more supervision. Some gave constructive examples of when supervision was beneficial... [two paragraphs of quaNT data]

- 'I'm quite happy with the general set up, knowing if I have a problem it can be sorted on the telephone.' (Respondent B)

(Fleming and Taylor, 2007, (pp67–76)

Contradicting responses from different sources on a similar topic are best presented together using both quantitative data as illustrated in the example below.

Example – Contradictory data from quantitative and qualitative sources

Preparation and goal setting emerged as essential aspects of observations in the qualitative data, particularly within a practice learning opportunity (PLO1). Quantitative findings indicate that the majority of students (n = 11) (92%) within PLO1 and (n = 10) (83%) within a practice learning opportunity (PLO2) were aware of goals being set prior to observations. This contrasts with the predominant practice teacher view that goals were set prior to each observation (n = 9) (100%).

(Irwin and McGlade, 2012, pp92–108)

As for all studies, the presentation of results in a mixed-methods study must make sense to the typical reader. The most important results may be presented first, or those that enable the study to be understood most readily, or those that relate to the central research question. Unexpected results might be presented early on if they are regarded as particularly important or statistically significant, or later on if they are being ascribed error or spurious circumstances. Another alternative is to order the results according to the findings from an over-arching question on the topic, such as is illustrated in the example below.

Example – Ordering of topics according to an over-arching question

'These topics and their sequence were derived from the rank order of the responses to the first section of the questionnaire, *reasons for considering leaving*. The first five themes were raised in the [comparable] Welsh study referred to above. The final topic of *job satisfaction* is a theme that emerged during the present study.'

(Fleming and Taylor, 2007, pp67–76)

Presentation of written materials

The sequence, layout, grammar, spelling and referencing are important so as to communicate clearly to your audience and to ensure readability. In this book we only refer in general terms to these matters, and the reader is referred to items in the Further reading section below for more detail. Similarly, due to our particular focus we cannot cover all aspects of writing articles for journals, and the interested reader is recommended to attend a short course on this. A few specific rules, important when writing the findings section, are highlighted here.

A sentence should contain no unnecessary words, a paragraph no unnecessary sentences and, for the same reason, a drawing should contain no unnecessary lines or unnecessary elements. Quantitative data is, by convention, most commonly presented as the number followed by the percentage in brackets (%) as in the example in Table 8.2. Ensure that you use consistent terminology throughout, in particular as to whether the study is research, audit or service evaluation for governance purposes (National Patient Safety Agency, 2010), and for any theoretical concepts and for terms defined in statute or in regulations. Any references to illustrations such as tables or figures should be clear and consistent, as these guide the reader to another format thought necessary for illustrating a point made in the text.

Summary

- Presentations about research, professional audit and service evaluation projects have a standard structure: context, methods, results (or findings) and discussion. However, the depth in which you cover each of these must be adapted to the audience.
- It is essential to be clear on your audience, whether for a written or oral presentation, and to relate your message to the audience. This is how you decide on the mode of communication and the amount of detail to include on each element.
- Ensure that the paper or oral presentation has a clear structure and logical development which uses signposting and link phrases to connect the key parts.

- Use visuals as appropriate for efficient presentation of data.
- Present a summary of the data or respondents at the start of the *results* or *findings* section. Include limitations of the study at the start of the *discussion* section.
- Note the conventions for referencing and grammatical presentation; they make research much more readable.
- There is an extensive body of literature on the crafts of writing and making presentations, beyond the scope of this book.

Further reading

Fink, A (2002) *How to Report on Surveys*, London: Sage.

This book gives useful illustrations of data presentation including visual aspects.

Bazeley, P (2013) *Qualitative Data Analysis: Practical Strategies*, London: Sage.

This useful book on analysis of qualitative data contains helpful points on presentation.

OSCOLA referencing system for statutes and case law may be found at: www.law.ox.ac.uk/publications/oscola.php

Pallant, J (2013) *SPSS Survival Manual: A Step by Step Guide to Data Analysis using IBM SPSS for Windows* (5th edition), Buckingham: Open University Press.

This excellent book gives clear and accurate guidance on standard presentation of the results of statistical tests.

Szuchman, LT and Thomlison, B (2011) *Writing With Style: APA Style for Social Work*, Belmont, CA: Brooks-Cole.

This is a useful book for understanding the most common version of Harvard referencing that is in use, that used by the American Psychological Association, in a presentation designed for social workers. APA version of Harvard is standard for many journals in social sciences.

University of Ulster (2012) Faculty of Social Sciences http://library.ulster.ac.uk/soc/harvard.pdf

This University of Ulster website provides a very useful guide to Harvard referencing.

9: Drawing out the Discussion, Conclusions and Recommendations

Chapter aims

This chapter will:

- guide you in constructing the *discussion* and *conclusions* sections of your report or oral presentation, where the results or findings must be related to:
    - the context of the study;
    - previous research on the topic; and
    - the theoretical foundation for the study.
- illustrate how to highlight the main findings and outline limitations of the study;
- show how to link the study findings to contextual factors such as law, policy, standards and service development strategies;
- illustrate the interplay between theoretical conceptualisations and empirical studies as feeding each other in creating knowledge for professional practice;
- show how to draw out conclusions and recommendations soundly based on the study results;
- illustrate key aspects using examples from social work research.

Structure of the discussion section

The discussion section of your report or oral presentation tells the story and, as such, it is often considered the most important part of a study. It should be built soundly on the evidence generated by your study, and demonstrate the correctness of the interpretation of the results or findings. It should have an underlying authority in its tone based on the evidence generated by the study, but drawing out the implications of the results or findings. The discussion section must have a logical reasoning process, and demonstrate the robustness of the results by their connection to earlier contextual parts of the report. It is essential that the discussion is soundly rooted in the study results and findings, and that it does not indulge in groundless speculation.

Be aware of the wording of your report or oral presentation, particularly in the discussion, conclusion and recommendations where there is the greatest temptation to include unnecessary material or clumsy, offensive wording. It is important to be concise and clear avoiding any temptation to use jargon. Be aware of 'politics' (with a small 'p'), whether you are undertaking the project as an employee of the organisation where the study is based or as an outsider. Be aware that your report will probably be in the public domain. If you are undertaking this project as part of your work role, then bear in mind that your employer will probably have intellectual property rights and a veto on what goes into the public domain. This is rarely a problem if you have expressed reasonable criticism (and some praise!) and the project has been approached with the ultimate aim of improving practice with clients and families without intending to offend any particular individual, team, department or organisation.

By convention, the discussion section begins with an outline of the limitations of the project before going on to highlight the main findings. The discussion section will then go on to relate your study results or findings to the context, to previous research on the topic and to the theoretical basis of the study. However, the sequence of these later elements is more variable. The depth of coverage of these as well as their sequence will depend on the type of study. For example, a service evaluation is likely to focus primarily (and firstly) on the organisational and need context, and the theoretical base for the intervention being evaluated. By contrast, a research study with a more generalised purpose is likely to focus primarily (and firstly) on the relationship to previous research and the possible theoretical interpretations of the results. The discussion section leads the reader towards the conclusions and recommendations which may follow. These various elements are discussed below.

Limitations of the study

It is conventional to begin the discussion section with a paragraph outlining the limitations of the study. Some authors reporting on research for the first time struggle with this. This may seem a strange way to begin the discussion, but experience shows it is generally best. It feels even stranger to finish the discussion on a negative note by listing the limitations at the end! The results and findings of research, audit and service evaluation projects are used by those in leadership roles, whether as senior professionals, managers or policy makers, to inform their decisions (Taylor, 2013). It is important that readers of your report, or those listening to your presentation, are clear on the limitations to the study. You want to ensure that people place due, but not undue, reliance on the results presented.

It is usual, of course, to give some explanation for weaknesses identified, and give some mitigating factor that minimises the effect. If you are writing a journal article, note that some journals will expect you to make some comment about the characteristics of non-respondents in a survey, to indicate the extent to which those who responded may be regarded as typical of those invited to participate. It is common to have to report a response rate to a survey that is lower than desired. The response rate that statisticians regard as reasonable for a robust study that is not prone to undue error is often much higher than that achievable in surveys of busy professionals. An example of a paragraph on limitations of a survey is given below.

Example – Study limitations for a survey

The 41 per cent return rate was typical for surveys of busy professionals and is slightly higher than is often achieved. Possible contributory factors to the limited return may include concern by respondents about admitting a lack of knowledge of social care governance or a perceived lack of relevance. There was a wide range of respondents across client groups and roles including management and training, as well as practice. The Health and Social Care Trust in which the study took place is one of five serving Northern Ireland and was a convenience sample. This survey was five years after the introduction of *social care governance* and one year after the issue of the Social Care Governance Workbook.

(Taylor and Campbell, 2011, pp256–272)

This brief section on limitations of the study is usually one paragraph, and may note ways that others might improve on the method. You might also indicate topics for future research that were beyond the scope of this study due to resource constraints. Mitigating factors may be included such as in the example of a statement of limitations for a qualitative study given below.

Example – Study limitations for a qualitative study

This study focused on the perspectives of professionals involved in decision making about the long-term care of individual older people at home, not on the views of older people or their families. Access to staff was necessarily through their managers. This may have introduced some bias, perhaps tending to recruit those less critical of the employing organisation. However, in practice this tended to be arrangements such as permitting access to a particular team selected because they were not under undue workload pressure at that time and might be more enthusiastic about participating, or inviting participation from staff working in a range of teams

→

or settings. Although home care managers (who directly supervised home care workers) were study participants, it was unfortunately not possible in this study to gather the views of home care workers themselves. The study remit was wider than home care services, and participants included those who were involved in planning the delivery of the home care service, and who carried a responsibility for the care plan (and who might be blamed if harm ensued). It would be valuable to explore these issues with home care workers and with patients and clients. The study sample was limited to the 'core client group' of services for older people in general, but a study that included specialist services would have given a fuller picture. Nonetheless, most of the participants served older people with a wide range of health and social care needs.

(Taylor and Donnelly, 2006b, pp239–256)

When a study highlights the limitations of the study, good practice suggests you might also indicate topics from future research as shown in the example below.

Example – Study limitations with suggestions for future research

The main limitation of the study relates to the relatively small size, which means that gener-alisations are restricted. The 'elephant in the room' throughout all of the research has been the service user. Future research could focus on the issues raised in this study and report on how they are experienced by, and affect, service users. The role of supervision would also benefit from further research in terms of preparation and goal setting. The potential for observations to be included in the preparation for practice module of the social work degree could also be explored.

(Irwin and McGlade, 2012, pp92–108)

Highlight main findings of the study

The discussion section will highlight the main results or findings of the study. The sequence of topics might be structured in the same sequence as in the results section of your report or presentation. Alternatively, you might sequence the discussion according to their import for the particular audience. You should include an explanatory sentence to signpost the sequence of topics for the reader or listener at the start, particularly if you do not discuss them in the same sequence as in the results section.

There is a fine line to be drawn in terms of the extent to which the discussion section repeats the results of your study. The discussion needs to be firmly rooted in your study findings, but should not be repetitive of the results section. The discussion section needs to look ahead to drawing conclusions and recommendations and not simply summarise results. A general rule of thumb would be to minimise the reporting of numbers, such as reducing detailed scores to the most significant results, ensuring that this reporting is clearly linked to making a point (such as in relation to the context or previous research as discussed below) rather than simply repeating the data. The essence is to discuss the major issues from the results, rather than to reiterate them. An example is given below.

Example – Discussion of a major finding

In this article we described how well-constructed practical tools can enable a more detailed discussion between professionals and clients regarding risk issues thereby enabling a more sensitive health and social care response that also takes account of some of the realities of accountability and blame when harm occurs. These discussions help to manage more transparently the tension between the views of the individual clients – involving both aspirations and fears – and the responsibilities of the professional in relation to organisational management of risk. Supporting users of services in reasoned, reasonable risk-taking so as to achieve agreed care goals – such as increased independence – requires this risk dialogue to be facilitated.

(Taylor and McKeown, 2013, pp162–175)

Linking to the context of the study

A key dimension of the discussion section is to link the results or findings back to the context and reason for undertaking the study (see example below). This may be direct reference to the measured or perceived effect of a policy or regulation, or data on service provision or perceptions of services. If objectives have been set at the start of the project, then this is the place to discuss whether they have been met.

Example – Discussion section linking to study context

The results section of this service evaluation reported data on working hours of home care staff within an organisation, and qualitative comments by home care workers drawn from focus groups.

Extract from the discussion section: 'The increasing complexity of health and social care needs of patients and clients has necessitated a substantial change not only to the type of work undertaken by home care workers but the hours within which the services are delivered. This has resulted in a pattern of working hours that home care workers report as finding unsocial, unreliable and not conducive to family life. While the study found mixed responses in relation to working hours, the study highlighted the need for guaranteed hours as critical to the retention of home care workers.'

(Fleming and Taylor, 2007, pp66–76)

Linking the study to previous research

A task in the discussion section for any research project is relating the study to previous research on the topic. This is less applicable to audits and service evaluations where there will be a greater element of uniqueness rather than the generalisability of research. You should highlight ways in which your study confirms or contradicts the previous research. If you (or others) have conducted a synthesis or review of previous research, you can usefully relate your study findings to that synthesis. An example is given below.

Example – Linking findings to previous research

The study has highlighted the complexity of the direct observation process and the need for effective communication between all parties. Communication skills are viewed as essential components in the tool kit of a social worker and are taught on qualifying and post-qualifying programmes (Taylor et al, 2010). Qualitative data indicates that student anxiety reduces when an explicit structure is in place in addition to clear guidelines. The issue of utilising frameworks or models, and student awareness of this, therefore emphasises the importance of explicit dissemination of information. The findings indicate that the actual model or framework being used is not viewed as important. This particular finding resonates with Clapton's (2009) conclusions about models of placement teaching. It also resonates with the view held by Thompson (2011) that the key issues should be consistency and adherence to principles rather than slavishly pursuing uniformity.

Evidence gathered in the research indicates that students and practice teachers believe a widening of Humphrey's (2007) ideas on 'legitimate participation' is appropriate. There was evidence that practice teacher participation and intervention exceeded the parameters suggested by Humphrey's model. There was limited evidence of this being viewed as negative in actual practice situations. Students and practice teachers indicated potential disadvantages of intervention but none of these were cited in real practice scenarios. This is in contrast to a number of positive student views on actual incidents of practice teacher intervention. The key issues in these findings were that flexibility and professional discretion were viewed as positive practice teacher attributes within the observation process.

(Irwin and McGlade, 2012, pp9 –108)

Linking the study results to the previous empirical data is a way of ensuring that knowledge is built up consistently and coherently. You should highlight how your study confirms or contradicts some aspect of the accepted wisdom as previously understood from other studies so that social work can develop a fuller and richer knowledge base.

Linking to a theoretical framework

For research, as opposed to a service evaluation or audit, linking to a theory base will be a central feature of the discussion section. Research is normally situated within some paradigm or theoretical framework for viewing the situation, particularly if it is qualitative, as illustrated in the example below. In quantitative studies the context in terms of services and demography of needs is perhaps more prominent. In quantitative studies it may be the philosophy underpinning the policy or services or possible service development that is the underpinning theoretical framework.

Example – Linking findings to theory

Determining what was perceived as abusive behaviour requires an understanding of family dynamics. Chang and Moon (1997) noted how elderly Korean Americans' concept of elder abuse was based on their cultural norms relating to family relationships, including expectations of family obligation and loyalty. Hudson et al. (1999) and Mouton et al. (2005) have highlighted the influence of social expectations in family relationships that became abusive. Further inter-cultural discussion can be found in Phelan (2013). This emphasis on the psychological aspect of abuse being central presents particular challenges for professionals seeking to address issues of elder abuse. Concrete behaviours are more easily observed, documented, reported and adjudicated for their acceptability than intentions and emotions. Giving increased attention to emotional aspects will require higher levels of professional skill in areas such as effective communication with older people and understanding their perspective on the behaviours of concern (Killick and Taylor, 2009) as well as greater challenges in managing risk for professionals (Taylor, 2013). More attention may need to be given to psychosocial symptoms, such as anxiety and depression, as indicators of possible abuse.

(Taylor et al., 2014)

Empirical research is helpfully seen in the context of the inductive-deductive research cycle outlined in Chapter 4. Growth of knowledge to inform the profession is most productive through a dynamic interplay with empirical studies feeding theoretical development and theoretical concepts underpinning empirical research. This mutual dynamic is an area for development within social work and in other psychosocial research more generally. The linking to a theoretical framework is in effect discussing what this study adds to our conceptual knowledge on this topic, or where new areas of contradiction arise that need to be addressed in future studies. This part of the discussion can highlight identified gaps in our knowledge base to inform questions for future research.

Drawing conclusions

The discussion of your study results or findings in their context of their service context, previous research and theoretical approach needs to be drawn into conclusions whatever type of written and oral presentation you are undertaking. You should aim to achieve some sense of 'rounding off' or 'finale' to your piece of work. The conclusion allows the author to demonstrate that they have a thorough grasp of the implications for policy or practice. Arguably, the conclusion is the key part of report writing. Consequently, you will want to focus on the main message from your study, viewed in the broadest context where your study might be applicable. The first example below illustrates drawing the main conclusion in relation to service needs and the second illustrates drawing conclusions for an aspect of social work training.

Example – Concluding statement for practice

In this study, prospective adopters demonstrated some understanding of the theory support-ing post-adoption contact and showed a basic understanding and acceptance of the merits of some form of contact for all parties of the adoption triad. However, when focusing specifically on face-to-face contact with a birth parent they found it easier to identify the possible dis-advantages than advantages and they spoke with more conviction about these. In principle, prospective adopters understood that this type of contact could be beneficial, but when they balanced the possible benefits with what they perceived as the disadvantages or risks, they were cautious about how it would work out in practice.

(Turkington and Taylor, 2009, pp21–38)

The conclusion section should not include any new material ideas or concepts. If something is important enough to include then do so in the main text. The conclusion should not include references. It is also important that a conclusion is written with confidence; if the author and the reader were to meet at some stage in the future would the reader recall the key message? If you are drawing out recommendations, the conclusion should lead the reader towards these. Be particularly careful about overgeneralisations in drawing conclusions.

Example – Concluding statement for education and training

The research indicated a high quality level of practice teaching within the sample. Findings in relation to preparation, setting goals, intervention scenarios and student satisfaction with their practice teachers would support this conclusion. A number of areas would, however, benefit from further development including choosing observations, communication, and the timing of preparation. The key message is that what may seem obvious is not always obvious. Practice teachers should clearly articulate to students how they prepare, what they expect and when they may intervene.

(Irwin and McGlade, 2012, pp92–108)

Drawing out recommendations

You may draw out recommendations if you are writing a report about a study for an organisation. Recommendations tend to fall into two categories: (1) recommendations to the organisation where the study took place; and (2) recommendations for future studies. Organisational recommendations are prominent in service evaluations and audits. Recommendations for future studies are an important part of research studies, but are also often included in service evaluations and audits. So if you are writing an organisational report or presenting to colleagues in an organisation, you will need to draw out recommendations. By contrast, organisational recommendations are not common in a journal article because, by their nature, journal articles are written to be generalisable.

Organisational recommendations by their nature are intrinsically about the specific context where the study took place. From a service evaluation you are likely to be drawing out recommendations about service delivery systems, about training required, about information storage or transfer, and about 'where next' for the service area. An example is given below. For an audit these same dimensions may be important, but the focus will be on how the service can attain a higher standard against some benchmark. Ensure that your recommendations are specific enough to be understood by the readership, but not so specific that they cannot be substantiated by your findings. If your recommendations include mention of resource constraints, then you need to mention these in the discussion and conclusion sections also and show how they derive from the study findings. Most organisational recommendations relate to identified departments, teams or committees. You should not name individuals, but you could refer to a particular role if appropriate. You could, of course, check out your proposed wording of the recommendations with appropriate senior staff in the organisation before committing yourself to print!

Example – Drawing out organisational recommendations

Recommendations from an audit on social care governance [extract]:

1. The Trust should develop a social care governance strategy for social workers incorporating the findings of this study.

2. The Trust should provide training and development opportunities in relation to social care governance including the use of the risk register.

3. The use of the risk register should be subject to ongoing audit and evaluation.

(Campbell, 2008, pp66–67; cf. Taylor and Campbell, 2011)

⟶

Recommendations from an audit of referrals to a learning disability team [extract]:

A number of issues were highlighted by the study that should be addressed to improve services, including a greater focus on health status in first social work assessments, a review of case management practice in terms of case closure, and greater inclusion of 'newly diagnosed' adolescents and adults in service planning. The increase in recorded autism and reported behavioural difficulties needs to be included in service planning.

(Morrison et al., 2010, p173)

All types of projects, research, audits and service evaluations are likely to include recommendations about future studies in terms of a topic that builds on the present one, a repeat study to measure change (using the present study as a baseline), or an improvement in the method of doing the study based on the present experience.

Ensure that your recommendations are based on your findings. All assertions of fact must be documented in the report. Avoid the temptation to present recommendations based on your beliefs or biases that are not supported by the data that you have found through the study using its stated methods. If you are basing recommendations on related previous research rather than the present study, this needs to be stated clearly. It is best to strive to be value-free in stating recommendations, basing them on the facts of the study.

Summary

- The discussion section is arguably the most important part of a research paper.
- Its main function is to address the original question posed for the project, whether research, service evaluation or professional audit.
- It allows the researcher to demonstrate a critical appreciation of the topic and an ability to suggest creative solutions to issues using evidence based on interpretations of the findings. In other words, it tells you what the story of the results or findings actually mean.
- The discussion should be logical, coherent and concise.
- It identifies any weakness or limitations and comments, authoritatively rather than apologetically, on how these may affect the interpretation.
- For organisational reports include a few well thought-out recommendations including suggestions for further studies.

Further reading

Levin, P (2011) *Excellent Dissertations* (2nd edition). Milton Keynes: Open University Press.

This book is written with the student in mind and offers a number of tips and suggestions on how to write rigorously and precisely in a reader friendly way.

Morris, LL (1987) *How to Communicate Evaluation Findings*. New York: Sage.

This book is a useful guide providing a range of pointers and techniques to help increase reading ease. The advice is practical and highlights how best to provide an attractive and evocative report that matches the style of the audience.

Northey, M, Tepperman, L and Albanese, P (2012) *Making Sense: A Students' Guide to Research and Writing: Social Sciences*. Oxford: Oxford University Press.

The Making Sense series is comprised of four concise, readable guides to research and writing for use by students at all levels of undergraduate study. Designed especially for students in the social sciences, this book outlines general principles of grammar, punctuation, usage, and style.

References

Abdul-Quader, A, Heckathorn, H, McKnight, C, Bramson, H, Nemeth, C, Sabin, K, Gallagher, K and Des Jarlias, D (2006) Effectiveness of respondent driven sampling for recruiting drug users in New York City: Findings from a pilot study. *AIDS and Behavior, 9*, 403–408.

Agnew, A, Manktelow, R, Taylor, BJ and Jones, L (2010) Bereavement needs assessment in specialist palliative care settings: A review of the literature. *Palliative Medicine, 24(1),* 46–59.

Aine Morrison (2006) *Referrals to the North Belfast Learning Disability Social Work Team 1996–2005: MSc Dissertation*. Coleraine: University of Ulster.

Argyrous, G (2006) *Statistics for Research, with a guide to SPSS*. London: Sage.

ARK Northern Ireland: Access Research and Knowledge (www.ark.ac.uk).

Beart, S, Hardy, G and Buchan L (2004) Changing selves: A grounded theory account of belonging to a self-advocacy group for people with intellectual disabilities. *Journal of Applied Research in Intellectual Disabilities, 17(2),* 91.

Begley E, O'Brien M, Carter-Anand J, Killick C and Taylor B (2012) Older people's views of support services in response to elder abuse in communities across Ireland. *Quality in Ageing, 13(1),* 48–59.

Benton, DC and McCormack, D (2000) 'Reviewing and Evaluating the Literature' in Cormack, D (ed.) *The Research Process in Nursing*. Oxford: Blackwell Science.

Bergman, EML (2012) Finding citations to social work literature: the relative benefits of using 'Web of Science', 'Scopus' or 'Google Scholar'. *Journal of Academic Librarianship, 38(6),* 370–379.

Biernacki, P (1986) *Pathways from Heroin Addiction: Recovery Without Treatment*. Philadelphia: Temple University Press.

Boyatzis RE (1998) *Transforming Qualitative Information: Thematic Analysis and Code Development*. Thousand Oaks, California: Sage.

Bryman, A (2004) *Social Research Methods*. Oxford: OUP.

Burton, D (2000) *Research Training for Social Scientists*. London: Sage.

Campbell, A (in press) Interim report of ongoing study: A research evaluation of the well-woman BACP-registered counselling programme for Women.

Campbell, A (2004) *A pre-post evaluation of outcomes for drug related offenders in a prison setting*. Londonderry: University of Ulster.

Campbell, A (2015) *An Evaluation of Workers' Perception of Dual Diagnosis in a Northern Ireland Health and Social Care Trust*. Belfast: Queen's University Belfast.

Campbell, B (2008) *Social Care Governance: An Examination of the Knowledge and Practice of Social Workers within the South Eastern Health and Social Care Trust, Dissertation (MSc),* Coleraine, Northern Ireland: University of Ulster.

Centre for Reviews and Dissemination (2009) *Systematic Reviews: CRD's Guidance for Undertaking Reviews in Health Care.* York: University of York.

Chalmers, I and Altman, DG (eds.) (1995) *Systematic Reviews.* London: BMJ Publishing.

Chang J and Moon A. (1997) Korean American elderly's knowledge and perceptions of elder abuse. *Journal of Multicultural Social Work,* 6(1–2):139–154.

Charmaz, K (2006) *Constructing Grounded Theory: A Practical Guide Through Qualitative Analysis.* New York: Sage.

Clapton, G. (2009) *Stories and Lessons from a Study of the Enhancement of Learning Process on a Social Work Degree Programme.* Edinburgh: University of Edinburgh.

Coffey, A and Atkinson, P (1998) *Making Sense of Qualitative Data – Complementary Research Strategies.* London: Sage.

Cohen, J (1988) *Statistical Power Analysis for the Behavioural Sciences* (2nd edition). Hillsdale, NJ: Lawrence Erlbaum Associates.

Cohen, J. (1992). A power primer. *Psychological Bulletin, 112,* 155-159.

Cohen, J, Deblinger, E, Mannarino, A and Steer, R (2004) *Journal of the American Academy of Child Adolescent Psychiatry.* 2004, 43(4), 393–402.

Cooper, H (1998) *Synthesizing Research: A Guide for Literature Reviews.* New York: Sage.

Corbin, J and Strauss, AL (2008) *Basics of Qualitative Research: Techniques and Procedures for Developing Grounded Theory* (3rd edition). Thousand Oaks, CA: Sage.

Coren, E and Fisher, M (2006) *The Conduct of Systematic Research Reviews for SCIE Knowledge Reviews.* London: Social Care Institute for Excellence.

Crombie, I (2005) *The Pocket Guide to Critical Appraisal.* London: BMJ Publishing Group.

Currie, J and Widom, CS (2010) Long Term Consequences of Child Abuse and Neglect on Adult Economic Well Being. *Child Maltreatment,* 15(2), 111–120.

Darragh, E and Taylor, BJ (2008) 'Research and Reflective Practice' [Chapter 11, pp 148–160] in Higham, P (ed.) *Post Qualifying Social Work Practice.* London: Sage.

De Vaus, DA (1996) *Surveys in Social Research.* London: UCL Press.

Dempster, M (2003) 'Systematic Review', in Miller, RL and Brewer, JD (eds) *The A to Z of Social Research.* London: Sage.

Department of Health (2001) *Treatment Choice in Psychological Therapies and Counselling,* London.

di Gregorio, S (2000) 'Using Nvivo in your Literature Review'. London: Institute of Education (www.sdgassociates.com/downloads/literature_review.pdf).

Drisko, JW (1997) Strengthening qualitative studies and reports: Standards to promote academic integrity. *Journal of Social Work Education,* 33: 185–197.

Drisko, JW (1997) Strengthening qualitative studies and reports: Standards to enhance academic integrity. *Journal of Social Work Education,* 33: 1–13.

Duffy, M, Gillespie, K and Clark, DM (2007) Post-traumatic stress disorder in the context of terrorism and other civil conflict in Northern Ireland: randomised controlled trial. *British Medical Journal, 334 (7604),* 1147–1150.

Evans, GL (2013) A novice researcher's first walk through the maze of grounded theory: Rationalisation for classical grounded theory. *The Grounded Theory Review, 12(1),* 37–55. http://groundedtheoryreview.com/wp-content/uploads/2013/06/Gary-Evans-Rationalization-for-CGTfinal-2.pdf.

Fetterman, D (1998) *Ethnography.* London: Sage.

Fischer, J (1981) 'A Framework for Evaluating Empirical Research Reports' in Grinnell, R (ed.) *Social Work Research and Evaluation,* Itasca, IL: FE Peacock, reprinted in Fischer, J (2009) *Toward Evidence-Based Practice: Variations on a Theme.* Chicago, IL: Lyceum (pp191–192).

Fisher, M, Qureshi, H, Hardyman, W and Homewood, J (2006) *Using Qualitative Research in Systematic Reviews: Older People's Views of Hospital Discharge: SCIE Report 09.* London: Social Care Institute for Excellence.

Fleming, G and Taylor, BJ (2007) Battle on the home care front: Perceptions of home care workers of factors influencing staff retention. *Health & Social Care in the Community, 15(1)* 67–76.

Fleming, G and Taylor, BJ (2010) An evaluation of day support: A community rehabilitation service? *International Journal of Disability, Community and Rehabilitation, 9(1)* ISSN 1703-3381, www.ijdcr.ca/VOL09_01/articles/taylor.shtml.

Flick, U (2006) *An Introduction to Qualitative Research.* Thousand Oaks, CA: Sage.

Floersch J, Longhofer, J and Suskewick J (2014) The use of ethnography in social work research. *Qualitative Social Work, 13(1),* 3–7.

Franke, RH and Kaul, JD (1978) The Hawthorne experiments: First statistical interpretation. *American Sociological Review, 43,* 623–643.

Gerrish, K and Lacey, A (2006) *The Research Process in Nursing.* Oxford: Blackwell.

Glaser, B and Strauss, AL (1967) *The Discovery of Grounded Theory: Strategies for Qualitative Research.* New York: Aldine.

Grinnell, RM and Unrau, YA (2011) *Social Work Research and Evaluation: Foundations of Evidence-Based Practice* (9th edition). New York: Oxford University Press.

Hamilton, D (2012) *Incidence of Suicidal Ideation and Behaviour among Young People Known to 16+ Teams April 2011–April 2012, Dissertation (MSc)*. Coleraine, Northern Ireland: University of Ulster.

Hanley, B, Bradburn, J, Barnes, M, Evans, C, Goodare, H, Kelson, M, Kent, A, Oliver, S, Thomas, S and Wallcraft, J (2004) *Involving the Public in the NHS, Public Health, and Social Care Research: Briefing Notes for Researchers*. London: INVOLVE Support Unit.

Henry, G (1990) *Practical Sampling*. London: Sage.

Hollywood, M (2008) *The Impact of Restorative Practices on Residential Childcare Facilities within the Southern Health and Social Care Trust, Dissertation (MSc)*. Coleraine, Northern Ireland: University of Ulster.

Howitt, D and Cramer, D (2008) *Introduction to Research Methods in Psychology*. Essex: Pearson.

Humphrey, C. (2007) Observing students practice: Through the looking glass and beyond. *Social Work Education, 26 (7)*, 723-726

Irwin, M and McGlade, A (2012) You talkin' to me? Direct Observations: a complex process made easier by effective communication. *The Journal of Practice Teaching and Learning, 11 (2)*, 92–108.

Khan, KS, Rietter, G, Popay, J, Nixon, J and Kleijnen, J (2004) 'Stage II Conducting the Review – Phase 5: Study Quality Assessment', in Centre for Reviews and Dissemination, *Undertaking Systematic Reviews of Research on Effectiveness: CRD's Guidance for those Carrying Out or Commissioning Reviews Report Number 4* (2nd edition). York: Centre for Reviews and Dissemination.

Killick, C and Taylor, BJ (2009) Professional decision making on elder abuse: Systematic narrative review. *Journal of Elder Abuse and Neglect, 21,* 211–238.

Killick, C and Taylor, BJ (2012) Judgments of social care professionals on elder abuse referrals: A factorial survey. *British Journal of Social Work, 42(5),* 814–832.

Lipsey, MW and Wilson, DB (2001) *Practical Meta-Analysis*. Thousand Oaks, CA: Sage.

Macdonald, G (2003) *Using Systematic Reviews to Improve Social Care*. London: Social Care Institute for Excellence.

Malekinejad, M, Johnston, L, Kendall, C, Kerr, L, Rifkin, M and Rutherford. G (2008) Using respondent sampling methodology for HIV biological and behavioural surveillance in international settings: A systematic review, 12, 105–130.

Marzano, L, Hawton, K, Rivlin, A and Fazel, S (2011) Psychosocial influences on prisoner suicide: A case control study of near lethal self-harm in women prisoners. *Social Science and Medicine, 72,* 874–883.

McColgan, M and Campbell, A (2007) *A Survey of the Childcare Needs of Women in the Northwest of Ireland*. Londonderry: University of Ulster.

McColgan, M and Campbell, A (2012) *The Mental Health of Young People in the North West Region of NI, An Action Research Project*. Derry: Ulster University.

McFadden, P (2013) *Resilience and Burnout in Child Protection, (PhD Thesis)*, University of Ulster (p338).

McFadden, P, Taylor, BJ, Campbell, A and McQuilkin, J *(2012)* Systematically identifying relevant research: Case study on child protection social workers' resilience. *Research on Social Work Practice, 22(6),* 626–636.

McGlade, A (2007) *Developing an evaluative approach to assess the impact of a special visual assessment and treatment service on adults with a learning disability, (MPhil Thesis)*. University of Ulster.

McKenna, HP et al. (2006) Surveys. In: Gerrish, K, Lacey, A (eds) *The Research Process in Nursing* (5th edition). Oxford: Blackwell Publishing.

McSherry, D, Larkin, E, Fargas, M, Kelly, G and Robinson, C (2008) *Care Pathways and Outcomes*. Belfast: Institute for Child Care Research, Queen's University Belfast.

Medical Research Council (2008) *Developing and Evaluating Complex Interventions*. London: MRC.

Morrison, A (2006) *Referrals to the North Belfast Learning Disability Social Work Team 1996–2005: MSc Dissertation*. Coleraine: University of Ulster.

Morrison, A, Bickerstaff, D and Taylor, BJ (2010) Referrals to a learning disability social work team 1996 to 2005. *British Journal of Learning Disability, 38(3),* 168–174.

National Patient Safety Agency (National Research Ethics Service) (2010) *Defining Research*. London: NPSA.

Neil, E (2004) The Contact after Adoption Study: Face to face contact, in Neil, E and Howe, D (eds) *Contact in Adoption and Permanent Foster Care*. London: British Association for Adoption & Fostering.

Noblit, GW and Hare, RD (1988) *Meta-Ethnography: Synthesising Qualitative Studies*. New York: Sage.

Pallant, J (2013) *SPSS Survival Manual: A step by step guide to data analysis using SPSS*. Maidenhead: Open University Press.

Pawson, R, Boaz, A, Grayson, L, Long, A and Barnes, C (2003) *Types and Quality of Knowledge in Social Care, Knowledge Review 3*. London: Social Care Institute for Excellence.

Petticrew, M and Roberts, H (2006) *Systematic Reviews in the Social Sciences: A Practical Guide*. Oxford: Blackwell.

Ryburn, M. (1998) In whose best interests? – Post adoption contact with the birth family. *Child & Family Law Quarterly, 10(1),* 53–70.

Sandelowski, M and Barroso, J (2007) *Handbook for Synthesising Qualitative Research*. New York: Springer.

Sarantakos, S (2005) *Social Research.* Basingstoke: Palgrave Macmillan.

Sarantakos, S (2010) *Social Research*, Basingstoke: Macmillan.

Scott, I and Mazhindu, D (2005) *Statistics for Health Care Professionals: An Introduction.* London: Sage.

Shaw, I and Norton, M (2007) *The Kinds and Quality of Social Work Research in UK Universities (Using Knowledge in Social Care Report 17).* London: Social Care Institute for Excellence.

Shaw, I, Arksey H and Mullender, A (2004) *ESRC Research and Social Work and Social Care, Report 11.* London: Social Care Institute for Excellence.

Shulman L (2009) *The Skills of Helping Individuals, Families, Groups, and Communities (6th edition)*, Belmont, CA: Brooks-Cole.

Spencer, L, Ritchie, J, Lewis, J and Dillon, L (2003) *Quality in Qualitative Evaluation: A Framework for Assessing Research Evidence.* London: HMSO.

Starks, H and Trinidad, SB (2007) 'Choose your method: A comparison of phenomenology, discourse analysis and grounded theory', *Qualitative Health Research,* 17(10): 1372–1380.

Strauss, AL and Corbin, J (1990) *Basics of Qualitative Research: Grounded Theory Procedures and Techniques*, London: Sage.

Taylor, BJ (2003) 'Literature Searching' pp171–176, in Miller, R and Brewer, J (eds) *The A to Z of Social Research.* London: Sage.

Taylor, BJ (2004) *Risk in community care: professional decision making on the long-term care of older people: thesis (PhD)*, Belfast: Queen's University Belfast.

Taylor, BJ (2006) Risk management paradigms in health and social services for professional decision making on the long-term care of older people. *British Journal of Social Work, 36(8),* 1411–29.

Taylor, BJ (2009) Invited commentary on papers by Holden et al. and Shek on the quality of *Social Work Abstracts. Research on Social Work Practice, 19(3),* 366–369

Taylor, BJ (2012a) 'Intervention Research' (Chapter 27; pages 424–439) in Gray, M, Midgley, J and Webb, S (eds) *Social Work Handbook.* New York: Sage.

Taylor BJ (2012b) *Developing an integrated assessment tool for the health and social care of older people. British Journal of Social Work, 42(7),* 1293–1314.

Taylor, BJ (2013) *Professional Decision Making and Risk in Social Work* (2nd edition). Exeter: Learning Matters.

Taylor, BJ (Ed.) (2011) *Working with Aggression and Resistance in Social Work.* Exeter: Learning Matters.

Taylor, BJ and Campbell, B (2011) Quality, risk and governance: Social workers' perspectives. *International Journal of Leadership in Public Services, 7(4),* 256–272.

Taylor, BJ and Devine, T (1993) *Assessing Needs and Planning Care in Social Work*. Hampshire: Ashgate.

Taylor, BJ and Donnelly, M (2006a) Professional perspectives on decision making about the long-term care of older people. *British Journal Social Work, 36(5)*, 807–826.

Taylor, BJ and Donnelly, M (2006b) Risks to home care workers: Professional perspectives. *Health, Risk & Society, 8(3)*, 239–56.

Taylor, BJ and McKeown, C (2013) Assessing and managing risk with people with physical disabilities: The development of a safety checklist. *Health, Risk and Society*, 15(2), 162–175.

Taylor, BJ and Neill, A (2009) Sheltered housing and care for older people: Perspective of tenants and scheme managers. *Quality in Ageing: Policy, Practice and Research, 10(4)*, 18–28.

Taylor, BJ, Dempster, M and Donnelly, M (2003) Hidden gems: Systematically searching electronic databases for research publications for social work and social care. *British Journal of Social Work, 33(4)*, 423–439.

Taylor, BJ, Dempster, M and Donnelly, M (2007) Grading gems: Appraising the quality of research for social work and social care. *British Journal of Social Work, 37(2)*, 335–354.

Taylor, BJ, Killick, C and McGlade, A (2015) *Understanding and Using Research in Social Work*. London: Sage.

Taylor, BJ, Killick, C, O'Brien, M, Begley, E and Carter-Anand, J (2014) Older people's conceptualisation of elder abuse and neglect. *Journal of Elder Abuse and Neglect, 26(3)*, 223–243.

Taylor, BJ, McGilloway, S and Donnelly, M (2004) Preparing young adults with disability for employment. *Health & Social Care in the Community 12(2)*, 93–101.

Taylor, BJ, Mullineux, JC and Fleming, G (2010) Partnership, service needs and assessing competence in post qualifying education and training. *Social Work Education: The International Journal, 29(5)*, 475–489.

Taylor, BJ, Wylie, E, Dempster, M and Donnelly, M (2007) Systematically retrieving research: A case study evaluating seven databases. *Research on Social Work Practice, 17(6)*, 697–706.

Turkington, S and Taylor, BJ (2009) Post-adoption face-to-face contact with birth parents: Prospective adopters' views. *Child Care in Practice, 15(1)*, 21–38.

Williams, M and Paul Vogt, W (2011) *The Sage Handbook of Innovation in Social Research Methods*. London: Sage.

Wilson, G and Campbell, A (2013) Developing Social Work Education: Academic Perspectives. *British Journal of Social Work, 43(5)*, 1005–1023.

Index

Added to a page number 't' denotes a table.